CLOSER *than* BREATH

*How a near-death experience reset rejection
to limitless, unconditional love.*

A MEMOIR

by

Maria Coetzee *and* Louise Coetzee

Closer than Breath

Website: **www.louisecoetzee.com**

ISBN 978-0-6453497-0-2 (Paperback)
ISBN 978-0-6453497-1-9 (Hard cover)
ISBN 978-0-6453497-2-6 (E-Book)
ISBN 978-0-6453497-3-3 (Audiobook)

To Jesus–in whom we have our being.

TABLE OF CONTENTS

INTRODUCTION

We cannot pinpoint the exact moment we realised it (probably because we were too mesmerised with Jesus and what was happening), but somewhere along the journey, our hearts desired to capture some of the inexplicable and amazing moments, both the physical and spiritual, so that it could be reread and remembered by the kids and grandkids. A small journal to record messages to and from friends was the start, and then the notes multiplied too fast to keep up, so we transferred them to the laptop. Initially, we thought it would end up as a small PDF as part of our family collection. You know, the one you pull out when the kids ask about the events of the past and how it all played out. We were comfortable with the idea. It was small, private and easy.

'You should write a book!'

'Nah, but we are making notes for the kids to read one day.'

This was part of too many conversations to recall.

But then we never thought about the journey itself. It was never over. We never wrote the words 'The End'. The stories kept happening, so we kept writing. We are still writing.

We also never realised the impact the stories would have on others. It was personal as it happened to our family, yet the stories of the lives it touched meant so much as we listened to people talk about how different they viewed Jesus, how free they felt, how grateful they were for us sharing. That was when the penny dropped.

The journey we share in the pages of this book is not just a retelling of a series of events of someone else's story. No. We share it with delight and excitement because each of the learnings and everything encountered belongs to us all. To you.

What felt like the most horrific moment in our family's world turned out to be the best thing ever! We would like to invite you, as you read, to view things from inside our world, not as an onlooker but as a participant. What is true in terms of what we have access to, is as true for you. Our greatest desire for you who picks up this book is that the stories would touch your life and fill you with joy! That you will discover the spiritual dimensions that you have full access to, now. That you will enjoy the full life you have in Jesus!

With all our love,

Maria and Louise

PROLOGUE

This must be it. This is how I die.

I stood on the slope of the valley my husband and I were clearing for a dam. In slow motion, the next few seconds played in my mind's eye like a movie. The tree jerked to life as the tractor pulled it downhill. It rolled over and, as if alive, speared a defiant root into the ground. The rest of the tree became airborne, swung like a crane and whiplashed in my direction. *Surely what I thought I saw was not happening?* I turned to look back.

My heart sank.

Time ground to an agonising crawl.

My insides churned in denial.

It lasted only seconds, but those moments before the tree hit me were enough to initiate a tangle of prayers, hope, and denial, despite the quiet awareness deep inside that the moment of impact was speeding towards me. I could do nothing—that was the only sure thing—yet I hoped for a miracle. I had no idea of the effect it would have on me, my family, my life, the future—everything I knew to be real. I had always expected to meet Jesus when I died, but not like this. Nothing I had heard or read or learned about Jesus in my 58 years could have prepared me for this moment.

What followed was the discovery of a spiritual world so incredible it is impossible to capture in words.

As the tree swung towards me, I was overwhelmed by an urge to run. Since it had rained in the few days prior, the area was muddy and uneven. Fallen trees, waiting to be cleared, lay scattered, and the rough terrain made it difficult to escape. My legs could not fight the mud and holes to trek uphill out of the way. It was too late.

This is it then—a tree of all things.

THE WORM PLAN

I nestled closer into the branch's safety, my arms barely reaching halfway around its magnificence, my head low, huddled into my body. The armoured crust scraped my knees and arms, leaving tiny pink tracks, but I did not mind. The branches swayed gently, and the leaves hushed the voice of my mother. Our home in South Africa in 1965 had a larger than usual yard for the small town we lived in, which meant many hiding places for a six-year-old, but this was my favourite spot.

'Miemie!' She could not find me or see me here. My stomach tightened. I held my breath and kept quiet. Mum stood close to my tree, apron in hand, one arm on her hip, and muttered.

She will give up soon and go back inside, I told myself. I just needed to be patient. She called my name again, followed by a sharp tongue click. With a quick turn of her heels, she walked towards the back door and flicked her apron; the bounce of her dark locks reiterated her disdain. She knew where I was and that I could see her. That flick was her way of letting me know that she had not given up—not after what I had done.

I stretched my legs out on the branch and breathed out. A giggle burst from my lips, but my fingers failed to smother the sounds. I smiled.

The stunt replayed in my mind. This one made the top of my clever ideas' list! It topped hiding grasshoppers in my sister's toiletries bag, sand in her toothpaste, or spiders in her drawer. It was even better than the old bicycle tube in her bed. I would find the most vulgar-looking earthworms, the length of small snakes, and chase my sister, threatening to throw them down her back. She would run away, hysterical. Although my sister was nine years my senior, I believed I was in charge. I was the youngest of five; my three older brothers already married and starting their own lives.

That day, while my sister sat at the kitchen table, I'd concocted an ingenious idea. I picked a sage leaf from Mum's garden, rolled it tight between my fingers, then sneaked up behind her and dropped it down her back. It unrolled against her skin, and I knew its hairy texture would feel like a worm. I expected to be rewarded with terrifying screams. Instead, my sister sat there speechless and in shock. She barely breathed, and the horror on her face indicated she would not recover soon. I did not feel regret or shame, but fled the scene laughing, pleased my evil idea had worked.

Eventually, I climbed out of the tree and faced my mother. When I did, she gave me a decent hiding, one of many, resulting in zero behaviour change or compliance. Every time I hid in my sister's wardrobe with a pillowcase over my head, or grabbed her ankles from underneath her bed, or snuck up behind her while she hesitantly opened the wardrobe door, expecting me inside, she rewarded me with screams. Every single time, I fell to the floor, hysterical with laughter. And without fail, my mother would give me a hiding. I refused to cry, refused to provide her with the satisfaction of seeing me in pain. I would hide somewhere no one could see me, usually in my tree or on the roof, and cry. This happened daily, sometimes multiple times a day.

In a desperate attempt to try something different, my parents told me the story of an eerie hermit who lived in the mountains and never came into town. Apparently, he wore skins for clothes and ate naughty little children. They threatened to drop me off in the mountains if I did not stop teasing my sister.

'Oh, he won't eat me.' I shrugged my shoulders. I knew they would not let the scary man take me. 'You could drop me off at the poor hermit's place anytime. He is probably just lonely and would love my company.' A triumphant grin crept over my face as my parents' only response was a head shake followed by silence. I realised they were bluffing. The hermit was make-believe.

Today, I despise worms—any worms. There are no good-looking or cute ones. The mere sight of their little wriggling bodies sends shivers down my spine. They embody everything that produces feelings of horror. My kids snicker when I tell them that I teased my sister with worms when we were children. They tell me my fear of worms is my punishment for teasing.

If you asked me why I teased my sister with such relentlessness, I would probably not be able to answer. Even today, I wonder if it was because I wanted attention or if I was jealous of how perfect she was. My sister was any parent's dream child—courteous, reliable, and disciplined. To add to her impeccable behaviour was her gorgeous dark hair, large brown eyes, and dimples when she smiled. It was easy to boss her around as she was soft-spoken and tender-hearted.

Nothing my parents attempted could change my behaviour. Not until that day with the sage leaf.

Dad returned from work as the trees' shadows stretched thin and tall across the yard. After the hiding from Mum, I hid in my tree again and later watched while Dad walked into the house. The smell of dinner and Mum's high-pitched voice drifted from the house. Moments later, Dad filled the door frame.

'Miemie.' His voice was deep, and my name sounded like an unpleasant word.

'I'm coming!' I hastened down and scraped my elbow, but didn't notice until later. My painful backside, from the strap earlier, was far from my mind when Dad said I should sit on his knee. Sitting on Dad's knee when I did something wrong was worse than the strap. Tears stung the corners of my eyes. I pinched my lips together and refused to cry. He would not know how vulnerable I felt. I could not run or hide. *This was just another telling-off episode*, I told myself.

'Why do you tease my daughter so?' he asked. 'We have only been good to you. Your parents did not have the means to take care of you, so we took you in. We felt sorry for you, and in return, this is how you treat our daughter?'

Our daughter.

The words punctuated my mind. My sister was *their daughter*— their perfect daughter. I was not. She looked like my mum. I did not. I was not theirs. Not their daughter.

I stared at the photo frame at the far end of the room. It was decorated with two timber doves and held black and white photos of Mum and Dad when they were babies. Two pictures were placed together in a single frame, two who became one.

The kitchen clock's rhythmic tick-tock penetrated the walls and the furniture—brassy and triumphant—and filled my ears, my throat, and my tummy until it was the only sound in the world.

This is just another scolding, right? I told myself, but it felt different from the hermit story, different from the spankings and usual telling off.

Everything that once seemed solid became blurry as I tried to focus through the welled-up tears. My insides felt like hot melted wax. I was determined to conceal the turmoil inside. I swallowed hard and tried to keep my face expressionless.

'Where am I from? Where are my parents from?' I tried to control my voice, sound monotone, but the words felt shaky. If this was real, I would know. I would ask my questions and get my answers.

'Potchefstroom.' He answered frankly. The name lingered above my head and gradually faded. I felt compelled to fill the silence.

'May I meet them—my real parents?' My chin quivered as I spoke the words which felt foreign on my tongue.

'It is against the law. When someone is adopted, the register is sealed.' He pressed his lips together for a moment. 'It is for their own protection.'

The last rays of sunlight tickled the dust specks around us as dusk seeped through the curtains. In a few seconds, all the colours drained from the room.

Was this just a nightmare I would wake from soon? A trick of the mind? Something that could happen to someone else while I watched from afar?

Only later that night, as I pulled my blankets tight under my chin and hid in the familiar darkness of my room, did my mind form the words I never thought I would; replayed them like an echo that would not settle—over and over and over.

I was adopted.

The sun rose again the following morning. The pigeons sat on the telephone wires and cooed as usual. Did they not hear my news? My morning routine spilled into Mum's garden. Tiger, my scrawny kitten, purred and bunted against my back, its fur a dull ginger, like the colour of a washed-out dress that used to be a favourite. I picked it up and sat it on my lap, ran my fingers through its soft coat. I thought back to the day I pulled it from the stormwater pipe, half-drowned. Its coat looked more like something had chewed it and decided to spit it out. It yowled and clawed onto my arm, desperate to escape the water. Flea-invested and with bewildered eyes, she smelled musky—the kind of smell that lingers in your nostrils longer than it should. I did not care the day I rescued her, and I still did not care. I hugged her close to my face; my heart again overwhelmed by her helplessness and vulnerability. With my heart in my throat, I cuddled Tiger into my neck. My tears left a wet patch on her coat.

The air pushed against my skin, fanned my blonde hair into a golden dancing skirt, and disturbed the dust. A few seconds later, the wind abandoned Tiger and me. The dust swirl settled around us. My beloved tree swayed and beckoned with its arms open, waiting. I was not so sure if the tree was mine any longer.

The truth hung like lead sinkers from the bottom of my heart. My dad, my mum—they were not mine. I was not theirs. I felt conscious of the space I was occupying, like I had to be careful not to take up too much, just enough to breathe.

I heard footsteps and looked up. My sister walked towards the vegetable garden, picked a tomato, placed it in the rattan basket, and then smiled at me. I looked away to avoid eye contact. How was I meant to look at her now? She was not my real sister. Who was she to me then? Maybe she was just loaned—a loaned sister.

Despite my age, I did not overlook the perplexing idea that grace was extended to me, that it landed in my lap, and that I was obligated to treasure it. Because I was not their daughter, and my sister was, I pulled my head in and stopped the teasing. How could I not? I dared not toy with the grace that now seemed so fragile. On multiple occasions, my parents have told me how discouraged they were. My mind imagined what the most likely next step would be, and a chill ran down my spine. What if they got so discouraged that they would take me back to the orphanage? What if they did not want me anymore?

On the other hand, I despised the idea of being pitied. *We felt sorry for you.* I did not want to be 'felt sorry' for. I did not want to be the lost kitten rescued from the stormwater drain. I did not want pity; neither did I want to be vulnerable. For the first time, I noticed the strange feeling of the day's colour. There was something different, but I could not pinpoint it—like something had shifted.

My world had changed, thanks to a worm.

THE FURY OF WATER

'Wow, Dad, that must have been so funny to see. What else did Oupa do?'

At age nine, I loved to ask my dad about his childhood. He would relay the curious events full of vigour, and when he chuckled, it was a low hum that bounced like a swift-footed deer brushing the floor of our garage ever so slightly before disappearing into the peachy afternoon. I would tilt my head back and laugh from my belly, unreserved, letting our laughter's melody flow over me like honey.

'I'll tell you about the time he broke in a couple of horses, but first pass me that spanner, please.'

I passed the tool on and Dad adjusted something on the tractor. I listened with intent and watched as the words bubbled over his lips, somewhere from deep inside a well of kindness and strength.

'Miemie, you're doing such a great job.' He held my gaze for a second. 'I'm proud of you.'

My heart swelled. The knowledge that I could help this wonderful man who took me in, that I could make life just that little better for him, flooded my insides like the warmth from a fire during winter. Moments like these created a short vacation in my mind. If I could, I would capture these times we had together on a film, start the spool and never let it stop. I would let the light focus on the image while the rest of the world faded to a dark grey so that I could relive every drop of sweetness at will.

Every other moment was a reminder that the life I had was by grace alone, that I only borrowed the time with my dad. I was the only child still at home, as my sister had also graduated and moved away. So naturally, their household duties fell to me, even the outdoor jobs my brothers used to tend to when living at home. Winters in the Highveld in South Africa were bitterly cold, and I needed to clean the coal stove before I left for school—this was my service in exchange for food. The floors needed to be swept and mopped. I cleaned the house, and in doing so, paid my dues for the roof over my head and the clothes keeping the cold from my skinny body. Every other duty bore the same burden of something owed. At least, this was the way I saw things. The chill of winter made my fingers stiff, as if manifesting the retaliation inside of me.

'Piet! Miemie!' My thoughts were interrupted when Mum called from the back door. I crawled out from underneath the tractor, while Dad wiped his hands on a rag that had seen better days. Her footsteps were brisk and eager. 'We have a visitor.' She looked at Dad and then at me. 'The pastor's here. Hurry up!' She signalled and walked towards the door. We followed her inside.

Regular home visits from the pastor to collect for the church were not unusual, although often unannounced. We were faithful churchgoers and would do the right thing, by God and by people. It was our due diligence as a God-fearing family.

As expected from a young lady, I greeted the pastor politely, but felt conscious of my oversized overalls covered in oil. I offered a bashful smile and excused myself to get cleaned up. Not that I would make an appearance again, as children were not allowed in the living room amongst adults. At least not me. My sister would have been invited to sit with the adults when she was still at home, but I got it—she was their daughter, she was pretty and well-behaved, and she was older than me. People liked her. I envisaged for a moment what it would feel like to sit with the adults and talk about whatever they talk about, promptly dismissed the thought with a short snort, but then froze with eyes widened at my first glance in the bathroom mirror.

Not only were my hands and overalls spotted with oil and grime, but a stroke of oil was painted from the side of my face deep into my hair. My eyes widened even further. What would the pastor think of me? A girl was meant to be seen in dresses, clean and tidy, and here I was covered in oil. Stained. I looked at the girl in the mirror, tiny-framed, porcelain skin, fine strands of white hair around her face, and an audacious sparkle in her green eyes. I found the grimy contrast amusing, and a trickle of laughter exploded over my lips. I covered my mouth to mask the sound, only to realise I had added more black to the white canvas of my face.

I am sure they could hear the high-pitched laughter from the bathroom, but it was all right. This nine-year-old missy was born to someone else, and I was different. That was all right with me. I did not have my dad's wide-open blue eyes that reminded me of a cloudless day, nor did I have my mum's stern brown eyes or gorgeous dark hair like my sister. I had someone else's eyes, nose, and someone else's hair colour. Perhaps I inherited my cheekiness from my real dad? Did they love me? Would they love me now? With all of my flaws and my skinny legs? But they were not here. The girl in the mirror was the only one present. Although it was clear that I would never grow dark brown curls or look through gorgeous brown eyes at the world, I could be helpful. Yes, I was alone—alone to fight my own battles—but I could be there for the dad who adopted me. I knew how to be strong. I knew I could reverse some of the disappointment of who I was for my dad. I could be good. I could make something of myself. I could mean something.

The greenish-brown body of water called the Vaal River does not match its name. Vaal is Dutch for 'dull', referring to the water's colour. For me, its memories are anything but dull.

Our house in Meyerville was a block away from the river, which allowed for quick access to water sports like waterskiing—at its best when the river was in flood and wild. Since I was young, afternoons were filled with adventures and times of escape on the river, our playground. Dad would sit behind the steering wheel of our little red boat, the *Hawaii Kai*, and my tummy would flutter in excitement. I'd keep a towel wrapped over my swimmers, so that the expectant eyes of the crowd wouldn't focus on my skinny legs and awkward tallness. I'd walk to the jetty, get the single ski on, and ready myself. In a last-second attempt to distract the onlookers' eyes from my skinny figure, I would fling the towel towards the riverbank in their direction in the hope that somehow it would cover their faces as Dad pushed the boat into gear and I took off. The exhilaration and freedom as I glided across the water was something that was deeply edged into my being, as if I was made for that. I was known for my wild tricks on the river, some that the young guys refused to attempt. Back then, we did not have a long list of risk assessments. It was still okay to climb trees, build treehouses, and swing from ropes into the river. And yes, we did get up to much mischief, but we lived life to the fullest and look—I survived!

Yet the river could also bring heartache. The banks were laced with ancient willow trees swaying in the breeze. Their branches hung low like tassels on the end of a long dress, gently touching the water as it flowed past. If you listened, you could hear the rush of the wind whisper stories through the branches—stories from long ago and stories from this morning. The willow trees were both graceful and alluring, like a Venus flytrap. Those tassels had seen many people entangled, and sadly drowned on occasion.

As we owned a boat, Dad and I would often be the first on the scene when someone was in trouble. Our intention was always to rescue someone's loved one, but it was sometimes too late. I often wondered how people managed to get themselves in a pickle like that. Were they just ignorant of the danger or too drunk for common sense? The best feeling was the warmth that filled our hearts when we could return someone safely to their families, who would embrace them, thankful. The tears they cried would touch something deep inside me—the connection, the relationships, a future of togetherness and belonging that had been returned to them. That has, and will always, strike a very deep nerve inside me.

The river changed regardless of the season and could be tranquil one moment and furious the next—ask anyone who had witnessed a flood before the Grootdraai Dam was built. A thundering rumble was the first sign of the imminent wall of water soon to engulf everything in its path. Homes and businesses in the low-lying areas would often have nothing more than a roof left above the waterline. Most of the buildings were constructed of brick and stone and did not get swept away, unlike the homes built today from gyprock, but the devastation left in the wake of the flood was nevertheless gut-wrenching, no matter how many times you witnessed it.

One afternoon, when the river was showing its fury, two police officers knocked on our door. It was not an unusual sight, as my dad was well-known in the community, so we knew immediately that they were there to ask for help. After the usual exchange of greetings, one officer explained, 'It is an elderly gentleman, his children are worried.'

Dad wasted no time and got the boat out of the garage. We were the older man's last hope, as the police could not reach his house.

I always went with Dad, as I wanted to be useful. We reached the water's edge, half a block closer than usual, and launched *Hawaii Kai*. My stomach muscles tightened as we weaved in between the trees and rooftops surrounded by the brown mass that rushed past us. More and more water seemed to come from nowhere; the river paraded its plunder past us—a green bucket, plastic bags, clothing, a dog kennel. We dodged people's lives, and my stomach felt raw as I tried to choke down the lump in my throat.

We found the small house, the roof the only visible sign that it was still there. I took a sharp breath and looked at Dad. We were both thinking the same thing but did not dare speak it. Dad navigated the boat to the lower side of the roof and tied it to the house. He climbed onto the roof, and for a moment, I wondered how he was going to get inside as we had no tools on the boat. Dad gripped the side of a corrugated roof sheet and peeled it away like a sardine can. I just stared at him. He glanced at me for a second. 'Stay put.'

Then he disappeared through the gap in the roof. I heard the plonk as he landed in the water further below, and I held my breath. Would he get out? If so, when? How? My mind flashed back to all those times we'd pulled some stranger from the river's clutches and into our boat's safety. All I wanted now was for my dad to be back in this boat, to be safe—for him to be returned to me.

The windows were still intact and, like most homes in South Africa, were secured by burglar bars with permanent fixtures. It was just a matter of time before the windows would shatter under the water pressure and flood the house. My knuckles turned white as I held onto the side of the boat. I listened.

'Don't worry. I'm going to get you out.' An older man answered Dad's muffled voice, and my heart skipped a beat. I prayed that they would be safe. I still had no idea how Dad planned to escape. The doors would be impossible to open because of the water pressure, and the only other option would be the roof. How would he get back to the top? And how would he do this with the elderly man? I wanted to climb onto the roof to peek through the hole, but my dad's instructions to stay put kept me glued to the boat's seat.

I breathed again when Dad finally emerged; a frail-looking gentleman hunched over his shoulder. I pulled on the rope to allow the boat to sit flush against the house, and Dad gently lowered the man into the boat. He was probably in his eighties and continually said, 'Thank you, thank you. You're good people. God bless you. Thank you.'

I could not stop the tears as my heart felt thankful that we could save him, yet overwhelmed at the thought that this frail man had to be vulnerable, so close to death. I smiled at him and held his trembling hand. More than anything, I felt thankful to have my dad back in the boat— returned to me. Dad started the boat, and we headed towards the boatshed where the police waited for us. I looked at the people, the tears and outstretched arms. My glance shifted from the audience to my dad, and I realised he belonged to all of this community. An incredible pride for him filled my heart as I thought how strong and brave he was. He was large in stature, broad shoulders, unusually tall, and he could swoop you up with one arm for a bear hug. But, most of all, he had such a beautiful heart; soft and caring. Deep inside, I felt the rush of gratefulness, and I knew that it was by grace alone I was blessed. And while my heart bulged with pride, it was overshadowed by a never-ending longing that this incredible man I called Dad could be my real dad.

3

BALANCING GRACE

My schoolbag's leather handle squeaked and pushed back onto the calluses on my fingers as my grip tightened. My high school textbooks were heavy, and it was easier to catch the bus most of the way home than walk the whole distance with the extra weight. I thanked the driver, shot through the bus doors, and started the brisk walk to our house. I looked at my wristwatch. It did mean I had to get back to school in a hurry. I only had fifteen minutes to get home, a few to get dressed, and then four kilometres to cover on the way back, but I could make it in time if I just kept moving.

'Hello, Mum!' I rushed into my bedroom. The textbooks' weight made my schoolbag land with a dull thud. I pulled the black school tunic over my head while simultaneously manoeuvring my right shoe off with my left foot. Through puffs, I finished getting dressed into my netball gear and dashed to the kitchen.

'Make sure you're back by five, okay.' Mum dried her hands on a tea towel.

'I will.' I grabbed a slice of bread and sprinted out the door. The rhythm of my *takkies* (plimsolls shoes) on the tar echoed a comfortable beat, and for a moment, I forgot about my self-consciousness. At sixteen, I enjoyed the ease with which my body moved—felt the vigour and liveliness in my muscles—and a new burst of energy propelled me forward. I felt thankful for the opportunities I was given and for my home in Meyerville. Life was not always easy in the 1970s. Even though we did not have much, I never went to bed hungry. It could have been so different for me. Ample reminders were scattered in the everyday, and I took notice as I thanked Jesus in my heart. As I turned the second corner, the tiny house down the street became my focus. It belonged to a family with five children; the second eldest girl and I would often walk to school together. You could tell they were doing it tough. They had no car. The kids had no bikes. They all walked to wherever they needed to go. They wore tattered shoes, and their school clothes were less than pristine. I often shared my sandwiches with her; otherwise, the soup kitchen at school would be her only option. I felt sorry for her and grateful. Grace. That was all that was between me and similar circumstances. Grace.

I picked up the pace as I started up the last hill. The school gates appeared as I topped the street, and I took a moment to catch my breath.

The senior netball coach was a tall man with a sturdy build.

'Ah great, you made it.' His eyes were soft as he smiled at me for a second. Then, he turned towards the netball court and gave a succinct double-clap. 'Let's go, A-Team!'

Everyone took their positions. My muscles tensed in anticipation. Finally, the whistle announced permission to perform, give my best and not feel that I was taking up space or breathing someone else's air. I meant something to this team.

I gave every ounce of energy over the next few minutes, blocking and scoring goals for my team. The goal attack was the obvious position for someone with my height and fitness.

'Half time!' The coach motioned me to the court's side as everyone reached for water bottles.

'Miemie, I don't have your permission slip for the tour yet,' he said.

Could he see the heaviness of my heart that tugged at my tear ducts? I hesitated for a second, then mustered every strand of bravery to keep a straight face. This issue was not his problem; this burning in my heart—this longing to be loved and belong. It was mine to deal with.

'My parents said I could not go on the tour, sir.' I wanted it to sound like a passing comment, such as *Nice weather we have today*, and then move on to the game, but he was not prepared to nod and smile at my response.

'But the team needs you. We cannot win without you. You know that.'

'Thank you, sir.' I stared at my feet, but he did not dismiss me as I had hoped.

'Is it all right if I make an appointment to see your parents?'

I looked up and frowned. 'But my dad said he wouldn't spend money on—'

'That does not matter. We will make a plan.' He nodded with raised eyebrows and maintained eye contact.

A few days later, I perched on the edge of the sofa. The tension in the living room and the tangled feelings inside me colluded, and I was sure if I tried to move, my feelings would spill into the open. I wished I could mind-read—Dad's mind in particular. He sat back on the sofa with his arms crossed over his chest. He was quiet. Was he listening? Or was it the kind of listening that actually meant he had already made up his mind? Or had he? I held my breath.

'Miemie is an exceptional netball player,' my coach explained. 'She is our key player, and we need her to win this tour.' His words permeated some deep part of me, and for a moment, it felt soothing before the tense atmosphere extinguished every trace of encouragement. Did my parents even hear those words? Did they mean anything to them? The tension pulled on my shoulders and hardened the muscles in my stomach. Dad sighed.

And as if on cue, the coach added, 'The school will cover the costs for her. So please let her come.'

I swallowed and pinched my lips together. I could feel the oxygen leave my head as my dad straightened his torso and moved forward slightly before saying the words that allowed me to breathe again. 'Okay, then.'

Is that it? That was all my dad said. The elation inside of me felt like a breath of fresh air that slammed into the obstruction of questions in my mind. Was it too much to congratulate me, say you are proud of me? Instead, I said, 'Thank you, Dad,' smiled and fought to ignore the tightness in my chest—a mingle of ecstatic relief and a pestilent questioning of my worthlessness.

Our time on tour was unforgettable. Although we did not take first prize, our second place in League exceeded the coach's expectations and ours. We were over the moon.

I wish I knew then what I know now. Then I could have told my sixteen-year-old self that I did not have to reason about whether I was worthy of congratulations or not. That I should not overthink my worth, whether I was too much or too little. Too much trouble, too little worth for a fuss, even if I excelled. That winning the tour was not going to change anyone's mind or gain me any acceptance. That winning the game was for me, not for them. That should be my focus. But of course, I could not tell myself any of this. So, I had to walk that road to learn the lesson.

It was Sunday. That meant church with services morning and evening. I could get through the morning service, even though it was more formal with the usual reading of the ten commandments. But the evening service? Ugh. It was a struggle for the entire hour. The observances had become so engrained, so predictable, so—. I dared not say it. God would surely punish me.

When the door at the front of the church opened, the reverend entered. His long black robe added a floating appearance to his steps. He paused in front of the pulpit steps, head bowed. He was probably praying. The same door produced a line of elders, all suited and formal. They made their way up the steps to the specially allocated seating on the left of the pulpit. And then the deacons followed in the same manner to the right. When they were seated, the reverend finished his prayer and made his way up the steps to the top of the pulpit. He stretched his hands out like someone offering a hug, his eyes closed, chin up. He prayed while all the men in the congregation stood.

We sang a psalm with organ accompaniment and then sat. The reverend read from the Bible and spoke in his familiar tone as only he could. The words sounded holy when he said them. You and I could read the same verse, but it wouldn't have quite the right ring, the solemness, the weightiness.

I glanced at Dad and Mum, dressed in their Sunday best. Mum's hat matched her dress, her hands were folded in her lap, nesting a white handkerchief with pink lace trim. Her fingers were in rest position, like soldiers, ready. Should I doze off, those fingers would produce a stinging pinch that seemed to last. So, I shuffled just enough to stay awake, but not too much to seem distracted. The timber pew ate into my backside, but the slight shuffle brought relief for a few minutes.

The sermon was about sin and wrong thoughts. The reverend read from Ephesians 6:2-3: 'Honour your father and mother, which is the first commandment with promise; that it may be well with you; and you may live long on the earth.' (NKJV)

I knew I had sinned many times. I wondered if God would punish me and if I would die because I did not honour my mother? I could hear her call my name, but I stayed hidden in the tree—many times over. And I grumbled under my breath when the cold stung my fingers before school while I cleaned the coal stove, did the garden work or cleaned the kitchen.

I knew I was rebellious and did not honour my parents. God would judge me for my sins.

The sermon dragged on, and my head became heavy. My inability to sit still, overcome by the fight to keep my eyes open and the sudden sting of the dreaded pinch, ripped me back into the church.

I adjusted my seating and let out a sigh of relief when the reverend dismissed us with the familiar blessing prayer.

Falling asleep in the church was surely a sin too.

THE COLOUR OF TOMORROW

I could feel it inch closer, bit by bit, as the empty squares on the calendar grew fewer towards the final day of school. The last day of school for my entire life! The thought felt surreal, but my focus did not linger there for too long, as I had my sights set on something more significant than graduating Matric. Freedom.

The possibilities and opportunities that awaited any young person about to finish school were exciting and nerve-racking all at once. But unlike anyone else, the new beginning also offered the gift of learning where I came from—who I truly was. If I could complete that one piece of the puzzle, I would be whole. I could move on and hopefully reconnect. I would be able to get rid of this 'thrown away' feeling that had haunted me all my life. Then, maybe, I could even feel loved.

My hand trembled as I spread the red dress over my bed. I tried to ignore the dismissive voice deep inside me, insistent that I was just an orphan, that my real name would not change anything. I searched weeks on end for the suitably-coloured fabric, mastered each stitch and found a silver belt to accessorise the outfit in the perfect way. It hugged my figure and bolstered me for what awaited. Finally, I was prepared for orientation at The University of Potchefstroom, for the new me, and dressed in red—my colour of hope—ready for a fresh start, freedom, and autonomy. I was ready to be loved.

Dad and I worked over the weekends, and some afternoons, to rebuild the Opel Manta car I'd bought for 500 Rand from the scrapyard. It would be ready in time for my eighteenth birthday when I could get my driver's license, and ideally, in time for university.

I almost fainted with excitement the day I passed my driver's test. I still chuckle when I remember the police officer who issued my license. He stamped the paperwork, hesitated, and then looked at me.

'I'm issuing this license, but you do not take any of your river tricks out on the road. Do you understand?'

The way he accentuated *any* with a dramatic pause made me realise he was serious. I nodded with a sweet smile and hoped to portray some degree of innocence and sincerity. Yet, I knew the warning was a last-ditch effort to exert his command, given our community interrelationship. I was ecstatic to have one more steppingstone towards my goal checked off the list!

During one of our car rebuilding sessions, Dad seemed more quiet than usual, and I could tell it was not the job at hand that occupied his thoughts.

'Is everything okay, Dad?'

The sound of the wrench hard at work was the only answer for a while, and then it stopped. He straightened his figure from underneath the bonnet of the car. The frown on his face was a question mark, and he seemed to look past me, outside the garage, somewhere beyond the trees, the horizon perhaps.

'Miemie ...' He wiped his hands, and the pause seemed long. Odd. Like he was thinking how to say whatever he needed to say. My mind raced. What was going on?

'Why do you want to study education; become a teacher?'

Strange. Dad would not usually question my motives or decisions. Did he not think my study choice was a good fit? My heart pounded as I formulated sentence after sentence in my mind to find a suitable explanation. The topic of adoption had not been mentioned since that day with the sage leaf, and I did not want to hurt him. But that horrible day had haunted me and was the exact reason for my study choice.

'Dad,' I said his name gently, quietly like it was something precious, 'you know how much I love you and Mum and how much I appreciate everything you have done for me, don't you?'

He nodded, but his frown deepened.

I tried again, decided to be more precise this time. 'Dad, if I become a teacher, I could apply to teach at the orphanage.' I moved a bit closer to him, within arm's length. I felt vulnerable and scared, but despite the feelings that alarmed me, I knew I had to make every effort to stay connected to him, make him see why.

He tilted his head and tightened his lips, and I could feel the words before he spoke. 'I don't understand.'

I glanced down for a second and took a deep breath, then looked into his eyes. 'They keep the registers at the orphanage. If I teach there, I will be able to see who my biological parents are.' Even though I formed the words with tenderness and care, it felt raw to hear them spoken aloud, even if it was my voice.

Dad pulled a chair closer and plopped down, his face pale and lips parted. He shook his head and looked down for a second and then straight into my eyes.

What was he thinking? I hoped he'd understand!

With his frown ever-deepening and a determination in his eyes, he took both my hands. 'But I *am* your real dad. And Mum *is* your real mum. A blood test will prove that.' Tears rolled down his cheeks, and the words shook his body. He took slow breaths. To see my dad in tears was hard to fathom; this strong man suddenly seemed broken.

In one horrendous moment, everything on my inside became too heavy, and I stiffened my legs to avoid them from buckling under me. The only job my clenched jaws were meant to do was prevent the turmoil inside of me from spilling into the garage in front of my dad. I felt like I was choking as two things simultaneously dawned on me; first, what had happened all those years before. Out of desperation to stop me from teasing my sister, my dad had attempted one more strategy to try and gain some level of peace. It worked.

Second, everything I'd built my goals and plans around was false—a lie. I felt cheated. The irony was that I finally had my wish granted at this moment in the garage—I was his daughter, after all. I was supposed to belong. I was supposed to feel loved, yet I felt betrayed.

I did not know what to do and felt so confused and angry at the same time. I collapsed into my dad's arms and sobbed into his neck. Years of blocked-up emotions and new feelings I had not known before spilled over his shirt, and the ambition and plans to teach vanished in a moment. I pulled away from my dad, wiped my face with the back of my hand, and sniffed, feeling empty and completely strange.

'I would have made a horrible teacher.' I tried to laugh, but uncontrollable tears shook my body. I felt gutted.

The red dress was never intended to discover a new side of me, a new beginning, or who I thought I might be. Neither was the silver belt going to bolster me with courage for a strange new start. I avoided my dad over the next few days.

I tried to keep busy with anything that meant we did not have to be in the same room. I was angry, and the betrayal burned in my gut, scaring me. He'd lied to me—years of lying. Even though no one ever spoke of my adoption after the sage leaf incident, he never corrected the misguided belief. For that, I felt cheated out of who I could have been—who I was supposed to be. I felt scared because the truth that day did not change the past or make me feel loved. It shattered all my plans and dreams, and I felt lost, unsure of the next step, what I should be doing with my life now that the truth obliterated my main goal. Was everything I'd planned in vain? Would it have been like this, this emptiness, if I had been adopted and discovered my birth parents? Would I have felt empty and not loved anyway? I could not understand my own emotions, and I tried to silence the questions ignited by my anger.

Eventually, I just tried to silence the anger. It was much better to focus on what I had control over, what I was able to do, what I could plan. Being focused, determined, and getting up when life got me down was what I was good at. I have always been able to look out for myself, go for what I wanted. A few days were not enough to change my mind about who I had become. Now that teaching was off the table, I realised how much I loved numbers, and I started to craft a new pathway towards a career in accounting. I was not that helpless little kitten.

DO YOU LIKE BLUE CHEESE?

I smiled at the smell of chlorine and the glimmer of sunshine that danced wildly on the pool's surface as my youth group friends enjoyed water polo. It was the perfect start to our annual weekend retreat. Around fifty of us usually met every Friday evening around games and activities arranged by the youth leaders. On Sundays, we studied the church's sacraments, with the culminating rite of confirmation at age sixteen as the goal. Although a serious affair, the participation and successful recital of the sacraments and profession of our faith was something worth celebrating with congregation members and proud family as witnesses. We remained youth members until marriage.

Confirmation also meant we could participate in communion every three months, something I did not take lightly, especially since the reverend taught from Corinthians, explaining that those who eat the bread and drink the cup of the Lord in an unworthy manner are guilty of sin, and that we should first examine ourselves before we partake. I had sinned many times, and I was unsure whether I had asked forgiveness for all of them, so I sometimes abstained. But I also read in John 6 that if we did not partake, we were not part of God, so then I would take communion, only to worry which sins I'd forgotten to confess. I couldn't win either way, but I decided to put my struggles aside so I could make the most of the weekend away.

That year, our youth leaders chose Die Eiland (*The Island*), a nature resort with swimming pools and various holiday activities, including mini-golf and horse riding. Based in the northern part of South Africa, it meant a warmer tropical climate with long summer days and plenty of sunshine—perfect weather to enjoy pool games. I dangled my legs in the water and looked across the pool at the multiple groups. Which team should I join?

Before I could commit, a guy broke position and swam in my direction. At first, I thought he was heading towards the steps to get out, but his strokes were strong and determined—too precise and focused for my liking. Surely, he was not coming over to talk to me? Guys do not speak to me. My heart beat a little faster as he closed in and I tried to keep my gaze on the game and where the ball was heading next, hoping that he would veer past me, that I was mistaken, that he'd misjudged the exit.

Although his strokes ceased when he reached the pool's side, the water unexpectedly splashed against my legs and I felt compelled to look as he rested his arms, folded on the edge, his eyes on me. This was not a misdirected exit; this was deliberate. His calm and collected demeanour portrayed the opposite of my internal dialogue. I slowly pulled my legs up against my body and folded my arms across my knees. Nobody looks at me, nobody sees me. Why was he here? Why was he looking? For goodness' sake, what if he wanted to strike up a conversation?

'Hey, Miemie.' I'd heard him speak at the youth group before, but I had never heard him say my name. How did he know my name? Who was he? All I could think was that I did not know his name, that I wanted the fluttering in my stomach to go away.

'Hey,' I said, forcing a smile.

He nudged towards my feet with his head, 'Wow, what are you doing with a set of toes like that?'

I felt my cheeks flush in an instant, the warmth rising from my chest up through my neck and over my face. Immediately I felt cheated by my inability to control the blushing and then furious that I'd made a bad situation even worse. Was it not enough to be embarrassed by this guy? There was nothing amiss with my toes! As much as I could, I aimed to keep my composure. If this was the only thing I could do, I would not let him see how I floundered through this.

'Excuse me; I need to go.' And with that, I got up and left with whatever dignity I still had intact. I expected him to laugh as I walked away, but he simply pushed back into the water and re-joined the game.

Could he be interested in me? I shook my head—what a silly thought. No guy is interested in me! My classmates have all been asked out on dates and romantic ventures, but I'd decided long ago that I was not pretty enough. Besides, the guys were terrified of my dad, who looked like he could kill with one strike, not that he ever would. If my dad was not scary enough, they were intimidated by my water skiing, tree climbing, or whatever outdoor challenges I tackled. They would rather stay away than be seen as unable to keep up.

If not interested in me, why then would this guy just want to chat? Nope. He must have been prodding to get some reaction from me. That must be it. I decided it was best to keep an eye out for him.

When I noticed the guys, including this guy, kicking the ball or engaged in something other than swimming, I dashed towards the pool. I loved the water and the competitiveness of the games and immersed myself in the fun. Then, out of nowhere, as I took a shot at the ball, I accidentally bumped into this guy and felt that instant blush again. I dove under the water to mask the embarrassment, furious at myself. How did I not notice him join the game? Why could I not suppress this bashfulness?

Despite my best avoidance efforts, he snuck up behind me in the line during dinner.

'Ah, the girl with the impressive toes.' He whispered across my shoulder, just loud enough for me to hear. He singled me out. I politely excused myself. I had to go to the ladies' room. Again.

For the remainder of the weekend, I surveyed every centimetre of space before joining any activities. If he appeared anywhere in the vicinity, I would find an excuse to leave with finesse.

The weekend ended much too soon, as I could have easily soaked up more sunshine and pool games. We waited with our packed bags, and our youth leaders directed us towards our transport.

It was my turn. 'Miemie, you're riding home with the Coetzee family.' I nodded respectfully and turned towards the vehicles.

There, standing next to the car, was *this* guy, smiling, holding the door for me. My ride home was with him and his family.

Oh Lord, this is going to be a long ride, I thought to myself. But, at least I had shoes on, so my toes were covered!

The car ride taught me that this guy called Louis had four sisters. Also, I strongly suspected that he had something to do with the arrangements around my lift home, as one of his sisters had to ride with someone else.

I bumped into one of Louis' sisters the next day and casually asked, 'What is Louis up to?'

'He left for the Army this morning.'

Her response left me with an inexplicable sadness that overwhelmed and confounded me. I had no reason to feel sad that this guy, whom I barely knew, had left. I had no reason to miss him, but I did, and I struggled to stop the tears.

I did not hear from him again. And then I forgot about him.

A few days later, Dad, Mum, and I were driving home in the afternoon when we noticed two ladies with a broken-down car on the side of the road. I cannot recall my dad ever passing by someone in need of help. We pulled over and could tell by their attire that they were members of

Lekker Gelowiges, a small religious group from the area, known for their strict conventions and seclusion from all outside the faith, similar in many ways to the Amish.

Dad had a look under the bonnet and worked out that something had broken and offered to tow the car back to our place. Towing in those years meant we could tie a rope to the car and pull it along. At home, Dad got the car into the garage and immediately started working on it.

'Have something to eat and drink.' Mum motioned from the kitchen door to the two ladies who stood outside looking slightly nervous.

'No, thank you, we're okay. We'll just wait here.' The lady with the blue eyes had a kind voice, and I understood her reluctance had something to do with their faith, but Mum insisted.

'Come on, I've already prepared the food, and there is plenty for all of us. Come in and have some while you wait.' Mum turned back into the kitchen as if it was a done deal, and the ladies followed.

Dad finished up with the car and joined us in the kitchen. 'You know,' he looked at the ladies, 'I have two cousins in the Lekker Gelowiges I have never met.'

This was the first I'd heard of it. Dad continued. 'All I know is their last name is Oosthuizen.'

The lady with the blue eyes audibly drew her breath in. 'But I am Oosthuizen. I am her. I am Cornelia Oosthuizen.'

It felt surreal to look at this lady who was a stranger only moments ago, and now she was family. I listened as the adults recalled names of grandparents, aunties and uncles, laughing and nodding as they recognised each one.

Auntie Cornelia took an instant liking to me. I do not know what she saw, but I think fondly of her to this day. She visited often, and one day, she introduced me to Kerneels, a tall, dark-haired man, obviously part of the faith. The dots connected when she said to Kerneels, 'This is my family; they're good people.'

A few weeks after graduation, we officially dated. I figured Kerneels did not have too many other options to choose from within the faith, and the matchmaking skills of Aunt Cornelia overcame the scary dad factor. He visited over weekends with flowers and chocolates, introduced me to his parents, and life seemed near perfect. Dating reflected much more of an olden day courtship in which physical relationship was taboo, so we held hands and spent time getting to know each other.

Three months passed, and the church youth leaders booked our annual youth camp early in the year. We could barely wait as they announced the venue was at Amanzimtoti, a beautiful coastal town in Kwazulu-Natal, with warm weather and sun-kissed beaches.

A small group of us decided to leave by midnight to make the most of the trip, and Kerneels visited until late that evening before the combi was due to pick me up. He lingered at the door, longer than usual, and held my hands. He looked worried.

'Please don't go.'

'Why not?' I was looking forward to spending time with my friends, and it was only for the weekend.

'I have a bad feeling about this trip. Just stay.'

'There's nothing to worry about.' I kissed him goodnight and watched as he drove off.

A few minutes later, I heard the rumble of an engine outside and grabbed my bag. The combi door slid open, and out jumped Louis, dressed in a safari suit.

'Hi, Miemie.' He looked more handsome than I remembered, and I hated that my bewildered feelings were obvious as I fumbled with my bag and hoped that the darkness of the night would disguise the sudden flush of red.

'You're sitting here,' he patted the seat and grinned, 'next to me.'

'No, I can't. I had a visitor until recently.'

'It's all arranged. You're sitting next to me.' He repeated as if he did not hear what I just said. It was common knowledge that a visitor at this hour meant I had a boyfriend.

'But...'

'In you get.'

When we arrived at youth camp, as per usual, I aimed to remain invisible, to hide my awkwardness. However, I soon discovered that no amount of 'lying low' was a match for Louis' confidence and boldness.

The ocean has always been a favourite place for me. I adore walks on the beach, and the sound of the crashing waves gives me the feeling of a fresh start.

A small group of us, which included Louis, decided to take a dip in the ocean. The waves' coolness washed away the tension from the trip, and I felt lighter. Swimming was my strong suit, so what happened next was unexpected and, to be honest, a bit humiliating. As I dived in under a crashing wave and came through the other side, I drew my breath, but instead of air, another wave crashed over me, and I felt the burning sensation of salty water down my nose and throat. Determined to get out of the predicament, I took another dive, and for a second time, instead of air, I swallowed more salty water as a third wave tumbled over me. My muscles tensed as I forced all my energy into swimming upwards towards oxygen. I could hear my heartbeat through the rushing sounds of the water, and it felt as if the ocean was swallowing me. I will never forget the feeling of that first human touch when Louis grabbed my hand and pulled me to safety. One moment I desperately struggled to get my head above water, and the next moment, I knew I would be okay. I stumbled out of the waves to the beach and tried to look composed. I failed miserably.

'Thanks,' I muttered and tried to avoid eye contact as Louis handed me a dry towel. A warm cup of tea and shower helped me look the world in the eye again. Louis was never far away, and suddenly, his offer to accompany me on beach walks was validated, welcomed.

'What do you like to do in your free time?' Louis leaned in to narrow the gap between us as we casually strolled, and I longed to forever remember the feeling of each sand-hugging footstep. A strange sensation of warmth flooded my skin, and I wondered if the slight weakness in my legs would worsen as we walked.

'Umm, skiing with my dad.' My eyes darted in his direction, but only for a second before my feet became my focus again. I bit my lower lip and prayed that I would not need to answer any deep questions.

'What is your favourite thing to eat?'

'Gouda cheese.' I answered almost too quickly. I really wanted to believe that Louis' acute sense of purpose somehow concealed my lack of eye contact and twitchiness.

'Oh.' Louis turned and walked backward on the beach, facing me, and I felt compelled to make eye contact. A sparkle seemed to dance in his eyes as he must have noticed the flush that crept across my cheeks. 'Do you like blue cheese?'

I squirmed and dodged to his right and stepped ahead. I hoped to regain the comfort of some personal space. 'Ah no, eew! Blue cheese is rotten cheese!'

'That is too bad.' He scoffed and waited for my response, and walked in step with me.

'Why?' I should have seen it coming, but I stepped right into this one.

'In a few years, there will be no more Gouda or any other sweet milk cheeses.' He made the statement in such a nonchalant manner I completely forgot about my awkwardness and looked at him with my head tilted.

'Really?'

'Really.' He gave an assured nod. 'We'll only have blue cheese to eat.' I studied his face and waited for a slight smile or anything that would hint at a tease, but his fixed stare and open posture disclosed nothing.

'Oh nonsense, how is that possible?' I stopped and turned towards him, my arms folded tightly across my chest and my lips pressed flat.

He stopped and faced me. 'Well, do you know how blue cheese is made?'

'No?' I relaxed my arms, and he started to walk again. I followed. This time I leaned towards him and listened with rapt attention, entirely intrigued by this man. He seemed so different from the other guys who just wanted to talk about cars and boxing.

Louis spoke with resolve. 'Raw milk is used to which they add a culture to help it set. The solids are then formed into a cheese wheel to which they add a very special bacteria cultivated in a laboratory in Switzerland. It is called Roquefort, and it is contained under stringent quarantine in the laboratory,' he continued. 'Recently, there was a breach of some sort, and the bacteria has escaped from the laboratory. No one knows exactly what happened.'

'Oh really. Why is that a concern?'

Without batting an eyelid, Louis continued the explanation, 'The bacteria must be kept under strict quarantine to prevent it from contaminating all cheeses. Now that it is out there, it is just a matter of time before all cheeses will be infected and eventually become blue cheese.'

My expression softened, and I let out a sigh and shook my head in disbelief. I felt devastated that my favourite sweet cheese would one day be gone for good and did not realise he was joking until after the trip.

The thought of beach walks with Louis made me feel both safe and alive. On one such beach walk, Louis took my hand without warning, and I yanked it back in protest.

'You can't hold my hand! I'm dating someone else.' Instead of backtracking, Louis turned towards me, looked me in the eyes, and with determination said, 'There are two types of girls, those you take on dates and those you marry.' He pointed at me and smiled, 'You are the girl I will marry.' Not a question, just a matter-of-fact statement.

6

LOVE DESPITE ME

Louis strutted into my parents' home smoking his pipe, and I was convinced that my dad would throw him out. He did not. No matter the topic, he spoke with such confidence and knowledge it left me infatuated, and I felt guilty.

'You can't come and see me. I am dating someone else.'

But then he called.

'Stop calling me. The guy I am dating has only been good to me. I can't do this to him.'

He agreed but then showed up at my workplace the following day.

'I can't stop thinking about you,' he said.

The next day and the next and the day after that were the same. He called during work hours and would visit every weeknight until I could not bear it any longer.

I broke it off with Kerneels and felt gutted for him. I decided I would not tell Louis, but he found out regardless and promptly arranged a date.

'I will not date you unless you can ski.'

'Okay then.'

'And I am not teaching you.'

Louis smiled, and a few days later, he was in the water with the skis my dad had loaned him. Dad found it exhilarating to see someone discover the thrills of skiing, so he was eager to help Louis. I do not recall if Dad knew about the challenge I set or not, but generally, a beginner is held in position in the water by someone else until they have the know-how. So, my dad's request was not uncommon.

'Miemie, hop in and hold Louis.'

'No,' I said with conviction. 'I'm not helping him. He needs to get this on his own.'

I made my way towards the steps leading to the river, and found a spot in full view as I readied myself for a good laugh. This was going to be fun to watch.

My dad had made the skis himself. There was no ski shop around to buy from, and no shows to watch to see what they were supposed to look like, so it took some trial and error to get them right. Dad bent the timber using water and clamps to form the front of the skis and old tyres for the shoes. Because I skied with one ski, he glued sand towards the back of the ski and painted over it to provide a rough surface for my foot to grip for steering. The skis were thin, much thinner than the ones you buy these days, which made them harder to steady, almost impossible for beginners.

'Keep your arms straight and your knees bent. Wait until you have enough speed before you try to get up.' With that, Dad got into the boat, and Louis bopped in the water, ski rope in hand, ready. The engine started, and from the concrete step, I could smell the petrol and water, and an involuntary thrill rushed through me.

The boat's nose lifted, and the river pushed white streams and bubbles on both sides of Louis. I could almost feel the strain on his arms and legs as he tried to steady himself, but his body twisted sideways. He held on in that position for much longer than I thought he would, and before he could lift out of the water, he fell. I laughed out loud.

My dad brought the boat back in, and Louis steadied himself.

'Let me try again, please,' he said to my dad.

I sat and watched. Most people give up after a couple of tries, as it's exhausting. The water-resistance and strain on the muscles are intense. He will give up.

Again, the roar of the engine. Instead of remaining in the water, Louis got up much too quickly this time. He fell. I laughed. This was probably it.

'One more time, please.'

Dad said something about him needing a rest, but Louis insisted. Although I did not expect it, I felt the thrill and joy so apparent on my dad's face when Louis got up and skied. He did it! Challenge accepted and accomplished.

At first, I did not want to admit that he could genuinely care about me, not to mention that he might love me. But he never felt threatened that I could ski better than him, that I could fix a car, climb trees, enjoy heights and challenges. The other guys avoided the river when I skied; he tackled the challenge head-on without help. Where the others seemed to fear my dad, he spoke with audacity. I fell in love with his witty sense of humour and gallantry.

Three months later, I looked over the rim of tomorrow into next month, next year, the next decade and envisioned a lifetime ahead. I reached for Louis' hand, and we exchanged smiles and dreams. The golden El Camino moved us closer to the next step in this process as John Denver entertained us on an 8-track tape with *Fly Away*. In South Africa in 1978, it was not just chivalrous; it was expected that you would ask your parents' permission before marrying. It was tradition. The previous evening with my parents had been successful, even though I thought it was hilarious. We'd spent the whole afternoon detailing the El Camino and then my dad's car, then moved inside as evening fell and engaged in small talk. Finally, as the evening progressed, procrastination was forced to a stop and replaced by instant courage when my mum announced she was going to bed. Louis started with, 'Sir—' and my dad interrupted without missing a beat, 'Yeeeessss, Louis.' Dad had expected the question all day. I did not dare to laugh before we were alone.

Enthusiastic after the 'Yes' we'd received from my parents, we were on our way to Louis' mum—to pop the same question and hopefully receive a similar result. Unfortunately, Louis' dad had passed away a few years before, so it was just his mum. The El Camino had no seatbelts, and my weight was no match against the smoothness of the leather seat. Louis grinned sneakily each time he made a sharp left turn—much sharper than necessary—and I promptly slid across the seat. I protested all the way and only stopped when I bumped into him. Without fail, a smug grin would break across his face while he continued steering as if nothing had happened. I would retreat to recover some of my dignity, only to find myself snuggled up against him as we turned the next corner. Resistance was futile, and I quickly learned that the more I struggled, the more Louis seemed to enjoy it. I shook my head and smiled. We felt the thrill of a young couple in love, and my heart danced at the thought that we could build a life together, be a family.

As I repositioned on the seat, my eye caught Standerskop Hill in the distance—a nature reserve—the highest feature in this part of the Highveld, which otherwise consisted of a quilt of farmland, mostly corn or wheat. The lack of trees added to the hill's prominence and my stress levels on the odd occasion. Nevertheless, I smiled and thought of the fun times our group of eight friends, including Louis, had here.

It was only recently that we'd all huddled close together on a cold winter's night to watch our lantern project float away. I always worried that it would not gain enough altitude as it soared in the hill's direction and imagined how we would either have to run away or face arson charges. We'd searched for thin cane from the Vaal River and had constructed the oversized lantern in someone's garage, with only tissue paper and glue to keep it as light as possible before adding the kerosene-drenched cotton ball. It took four people to lift it onto the back of the Ute. All eight of us enjoyed the sights, as cool air transfigured cane and tissue paper into a softly lit wonder from a fairy tale that floated away into the night sky—off to some mysterious destination. The lift-off platform would be anywhere level and open, such as the sports field. The moment it gained enough height, we would jump into our vehicles and follow it as far as we could go.

I could not resist a chuckle as I remembered the local newspaper, *The Advertiser*, reporting a strange UFO above Standerton, followed by the district paper, *Die Beeld*, claiming similar sightings. A few days ago, our local radio station reported sightings as far north as Bethal and as far South as Vrede. Both towns are around 60 kilometres away. Our adventures made the news, disguised as UFOs. We were delighted and found the whole spectacle amusing.

My reminiscence was interrupted as we pulled into Louis's mum's driveway, and silence replaced The Beach Boys' *Good Vibrations* as the engine stopped.

The mood in the house was different from what I had hoped, mostly after we asked for her blessing. I remember thinking about her dramatic response—the way she dropped back into the chair, how she almost fainted. I stood there and watched the scene unfold in front of us. *I will show you*, I thought to myself. *I will be the best wife, the best mother, and the best daughter-in-law*. I went to see her afterward to ask why. Why the disapproval? I so desperately wanted her just to give me a chance—to get to know me. Then she would see that I was a good person, that I loved Louis with all my heart. She would like me, approve of me, even love me. She simply said that I would never be good enough and that she did not need to provide a reason to a child.

The winter air could not chill our love or dreams as we vowed to be faithful to each other in March 1979. We moved into a two-bedroom home with ugly green bathroom tiles, but I could not care less about the colour. It was our place. It was a new beginning, and our future awaited with endless possibilities, like a blank canvas begging for paint.

I stepped back to adore my handiwork and smiled. Our living room boasted my handmade macramé, suspended from the ceiling, encasing a beautiful plant, something living, just like our marriage and the life ahead of us. The best thing about our new place was the stove. It was not a coal stove! I enjoyed cooking extravagant meals for Louis, maybe a little more than would be expected of a new bride.

My love for resolving challenges saw me promoted several times at work. I realised a formal degree would be the only way to achieve my accounting dreams in a management position, and I enrolled to study a Bachelor of Accounting.

During this time, I discovered we were expecting, and I was delighted. It could not have been much fun for my forty-year-old mother when she learned she was expecting me. I wanted to be different. I'd always hoped to have a child while still young, to be there for them and enjoy life with them. Now the life I'd dreamed was beginning to take shape.

Louise was born in 1980. She was premature, in the posterior position, and without scans, the doctor's choices were uninformed, and we both almost died. There was damage to her eyes, though we did not understand the implications of until much later. Despite not being able to hold her, as she was in an incubator, my heart felt like it was bursting with love. I could never have imagined that I could love another human being this way, and I remember saying to Louis that it would be unfair to have a second child as this one has taken up all the love in my heart.

In 1982, I learned that my heart had more love to give. Christoffel Andries Petrus was born, continuing Louis' family name. We were thrilled that we had a son, as Louis was the only male on his side of the family.

In 1986, Mia was born, and the doctor was surprised that a newborn could have an attitude the way she did. We were happy, and life was peachy.

We bought into a butchery partnership, but despite our best efforts, the business folded after a couple of trying years. We lost everything. It hit home when, amongst our other possessions, they carried my kids' beds from our home to be sold. I looked at the circumstances the way I have always looked at life. I was not a victim, and we would get back up again. I borrowed some money from my dad and bought a computer to start an accounting business. To me, life is what you make of it. The tough times are just facts, information, a starting point on the next journey, like an arrow pointing in the new direction we were supposed to go.

The only thing I hated about being pregnant was that I could not ski. However, we more than made up for that afterward, and the kids grew up believing that everyday life involved lots of boating and skiing. A favourite spot was the Ebenezer dam, built on the Letaba River in Limpopo near Tzaneen. Tucked between Haenertsberg and Magoebaskloof mountains, it is often covered in a mysterious mist, notorious for its unpredictable weather that creeps up without warning.

This Saturday morning was no different, as the sunrays danced on the mist that lingered on the edges of the dam when we launched the boat. After I had a go on the ski, Louis tied a large inflatable tractor tube to the ski rope. The kids had a bit of fun as they bopped across the water, and then Louis had a go. I steered the boat with sharp left and right turns in an attempt to throw him off the tube, which was always fun. Half the time, I would look ahead and half at Louis to see if my shots were successful. I noticed Louis' eyes widened and then realised, despite me making a sharp left turn away from the side of the dam, that the tube had no steering, and he was heading straight towards the recently cut trees. I panicked and immediately switched the engine off, but it had no effect. The tube made land, swiped across the grass and timber, and entered the water a few metres in, Louis still holding on. I laugh when I retell this, but at the time I thought I was putting him in hospital. We needed some warm coffee afterwards, and I profusely apologised and kept hugging Louis, who came away from the ordeal with a few minor scrapes and shredded swim shorts.

Later that day, as we were still enjoying the water, a hailstorm surprised us, and we rushed to the car to escape. The two younger kids huddled onto my lap, and I wrapped my arms around them, wishing that I could hold all three of my kids together if only I had more arms! They started to cry as the hail hammered the car.

'Shhh, it's okay. Don't cry. We're all together, and we're safe. It's just noisy hail,' I said.

As we huddled in our swimmers, dripping wet from the water, it struck me how blessed we were. My arms could not fit all the love I had to give. If I could freeze time, caption a moment in a photo album, this one would read, *'epiphany of love.'* I had a husband I adored, three kids of my own who I could love more than life despite my childhood. We were happy; we were a family; this was home for me.

I sometimes wonder how different things could have been. Not for me, but my mother-in-law. Despite my attempts to prove that I was good enough, I did not feel accepted by her. Each time we announced we were pregnant, I thought it would change things, but she told us we were irresponsible and selfish.

I do sometimes ask, *what if?* I know it is no good now, but I do wonder. My mother-in-law made her last wishes known on her death bed, including who should carry her coffin. She mentioned her five daughters and Marinda, the oldest granddaughter, should be assigned this task, and Louis gently corrected her, saying that she had four daughters (his four sisters), not five. I was never perceived as her daughter-in-law, never mind her daughter. Nevertheless, her response left a bittersweet emotion in my heart.

'No, I have five daughters, my four and Miemie.' It did not undo all those years, all the times I attempted and failed. At that moment, I could still feel that familiar voice deep inside me, almost devious—*this is just another of a string of incidents that proved I was not genuinely lovable.*

THE INVINCIBILITY OF GRACE

'What else can we do?' I did not expect an answer.

'I don't know.' Louis shook his head, his eyes glued on the road. 'We'll need to learn how to deal with a blind child.'

I did not want the words to stick, to sink in, to attach themselves to me. It felt like we were at the end of a cliff. We had done everything we knew, and now that we'd arrived, there was nowhere to go, nothing left to try.

'How did we get here in under two years?' I peered over my shoulder to the backseat. 'All three are asleep.'

'It really hit home for me today, Miemie. I mean, he is the best eye specialist we could find.' Louis gestured with his hand and returned it to the steering wheel with a loud snap.

'They're still asleep,' I said.

'And if he is the best, you'd think he would know what he is talking about, right?'

'I guess. I just wonder if there isn't anything else we could do? I know he said no surgery could fix her eyes, but moving to *Worcestor*? It means we have to move across the country, find new jobs, new everything. We'll have to uproot our lives.' I shuffled in my seat.

Louis sighed. 'He did say Louise should start at the school for the blind with the little bit of sight she has left, rather than when she is completely blind. And you know how quickly her eyes have deteriorated over the last few months.'

'Time is not on our side. I get it.' I looked at her again. 'She is only nine. Who could have imagined this was all caused during birth?'

And then, one afternoon in May, I allowed myself a glimmer of hope. We heard about a pastor who prayed for the sick, and there were many testimonies of healings. One last attempt. *What if...? What if it worked?* I caught myself thinking. *What if it did not?* I could not allow the thought to linger for too long. There was nothing else we could do. Having faith, believing that there could be one last chance—that was the only thing left. When I mentioned the pastor to Louis, I held my breath. I feared his reaction might be an immediate dismissal of the idea. Instead, he said yes, and it was like the window opened a bit, allowing a glimmer of light to shine on the hope in my heart.

We made plans to travel to Durban by car, and because the trip was over 900 kilometres, we would undertake part during the night and leave the last stretch for daylight. Night driving has never been my strong suit, so naturally, the task fell to Louis. A few days before the trip, Louis' back went into spasm, and I felt like crying. I could feel the last bit of hope slip away as there was no way he could drive in his condition. I do not recall the little prayer I shot up to the heavens, most likely something between a cry for help and asking why this door was being closed, but I remember thinking that I was not going to give up. Not yet, not while there was still some way. If there was, I would find it.

At work the next day, a new client of mine came in to collect his books, as I'd completed the feasibility analysis on the fish factory he planned to purchase. We talked through his options, and afterwards, I handed him the invoice. He offered to pay on the spot, and his wife started to write the cheque. He was thankful for the work done, and as he looked at the bill, he interrupted his wife and took the pen from her.

'What? This is ridiculous! I can't pay this.' I was shocked as I have always considered my bills reasonable. He wrote the cheque himself, ripped it from the chequebook, and handed it to me with a smile. Thankfulness bubbled up inside me. The cheque was more than double the invoice amount! I could not wait for the meeting to end so I could call Louis.

'Guess what? We can afford flights to Durban! We don't have to drive!'

After I ordered and paid for the flights, I felt undone as I realised the extra money we had was the exact amount needed to cover our flights. How well did God look after us! My heart just sang, *Thank you, thank you, thank you!*

On board the flight, I wrestled with my thoughts, *What if...?* I called Louise to my seat. She looked at me, and her eyes seemed so prominent through the thick prescription lenses. I tried to gather my thoughts.

'Louise, do you know where we are heading?'

'Yes, Durban.'

'Yes. And do you know what we're doing there?'

'Visiting Rintie?' Louise referred to my niece, Amarinda.

'Also, we're going to visit a church this weekend. There is a pastor who prays for people for healing.' My thoughts tripped over each other. I could not tell her that God *would* heal her. That could give her false hope, and she has been through so much already with all the teasing at school. I said the next best thing I could think of as I took her hand. 'There is a chance that Jesus could heal you.'

'Yippee! Then I'll never have to wear glasses again!' She smiled and returned to her seat. I felt overwhelmed, and tears started to flow. I could not say, *no, that will not happen.* Nor that it would! I just realised that a child's faith was different from that of an adult—no complicated reasoning or analysis, just taking it at face value without questions.

On Sunday morning, we stepped into the church building, and my stomach tightened. Church for us typically meant stained-glass windows, flowing organ music, neat rows of pews, a draped pulpit, and people dressed in their Sunday best making eye contact with a quiet nod, a whispered greeting here and there, before everyone would find their usual seats. This Sunday, church looked like a community hall with rows of plastic chairs and a stage stacked with musical instruments that included guitars and a drum set. I held my breath and glanced at the drums for a second. The hall was noisy. People chatted, some leaned over chairs, and others gathered in groups, laughed, and hugged.

We stood in the doorway and scanned the space for any available seats amongst the folks of mixed cultures in their casual wear. Our bewildered looks and formal attire added to our awkward handshakes, as we were heartily welcomed and asked where we were from, before being ushered in.

I breathed out as we sat down. Regardless of the strangeness of the service, I decided to try and relax and managed a tense smile. During worship, people clapped and lifted their hands. It felt awkward, but we joined in, nevertheless. And then the awkwardness melted away as we took in the atmosphere. I glanced in Louis' direction, and my heart warmed a little as he looked relaxed, and the kids seemed engaged. The sermon felt more like a chat with friends, and when it ended, the pastor called for anyone who needed prayer. Louis took Louise's hand, and they waited amongst a few others at the front of the church. The pastor prayed for each person, and although I could not hear the words, I could feel my heart in my throat.

After the service, we met the pastor at the baptismal pond—an outdoor cement bath at the back of the building. It was waist-deep, wide enough for at least three people, and accessible by steps. It was cold and rainy, and I was wet even before I stepped into the chilly water and was submerged and prayed over. Getting baptised was something we needed to do, something we'd wanted to do before we left home. During the baptism, people prophesied over Louis. I do not think he knew what was happening, but it did not matter. There was a fire in our bellies, and a new world had opened up for us.

After the baptism, we dried off, dressed, and it was time to head back to my niece Amarinda's place. They lived nearby and had joined us for the service, and witnessed the baptism. We all crammed into their car, and on the way to their house, Louis casually said, 'Hey, Louise, why don't you take off your glasses?'

Usually, when she removed her glasses, her eyes could not focus, and she could not see anything further than an arm's length away.

'Okay.' She shrugged, took her glasses off, and leaned forward to look past Amarinda and her daughter to see me on the furthest end of the car.

Louise screamed, 'Mummy! I can see you!'

I leaned forward and looked into her face. Goosebumps covered my body as she returned my gaze, eyes widened and, for the first time, entirely focused. Louis pulled over, and we burst out of the car.

Louise kept shouting, 'I can see! Look at the leaves! Look at the trees! I can see the sky and the clouds! Mummy, I can see you!'

We were overwhelmed with emotion, and still in shock and wonder, we laughed through tears. I felt so small, my heart an explosion of gratefulness. It was hard to grapple with the notion that the God of the universe would hear our prayer and answer it, that we were important enough for him to heal our daughter's eyes. I hugged her and cried and cried. We would look at something she pointed at and then cry again. There was no shame in tears; it was overflowing from the fullness in our hearts. God became real—very real. Where he'd seemed distant before, he was now interested in us, involved, and personal. We had to learn more, knew that there was more to discover than we thought.

Back at home, our reverend came to visit us.

'I am happy for you, I truly am, but the church board...' He sighed. 'Please, what if you just kept your baptism a secret? No one needs to know.'

I could feel the internal conflict the reverend tried to disguise and immediately understood that the doctrinal difference around baptism and his heart for people were at war.

'Reverend, with all respect, there is no way we could keep this quiet. It will bubble out if we strike up any conversation.'

He looked at the floor and sighed deeply. 'You are the only ones who bring a bit of life into the congregation. Louis will be stripped of his deaconship. You will be kicked out! Please?'

'We can't pretend. We're sorry,' I said.

After his car left our driveway, I turned to Louis.

'I can't be a submarine Christian—submerged only to pop up on Sundays.

'No regrets, my love.' He kissed me on the forehead and took my hand as we walked indoors. 'Whatever is burning in our hearts is stronger than both of us.'

We knew this was right. What others thought or our status at church seemed less important than the zeal we felt deep inside, something we could not quite grasp at the time.

Over the next few days, a never-ending need to share and connect with like-minded souls encouraged us to search for a church like the one we'd attended in Durban. We soon found a congregation and joined the morning service, then the evening session, and eventually all the available meetings during the week, including small groups, youth, and evangelical ministry. It was not long before we dedicated weekends to religious camps designed for families, marriages, for men or women. We did not mind what the theme was; we attended all we could. Enthralled, we felt like children who'd discovered a world that we did not know existed. Each time a visiting pastor, healer, or prophet was in the area, we were determined not to miss out on anything new that God was doing.

Before the catalyst—the healing and baptism—church had felt like a duty (not that we would have admitted it back then). It was something we had to do; it was expected of a good Christian to attend weekly. Deep inside, I was scared of God. Although he was loving, he was also a just God and would punish me if I took a wrong step. Over the next few weeks, I discovered that God was never the authoritarian I'd made him out to be. He was loving, kind, and gracious. It was not a theory; it was evident in how he cared for us and those whose lives he touched daily around us. We wanted to know all we could and eagerly devoured everything we could lay our hands on—books, teachings, seminars, and tapes.

We discovered an intimate and personal God, and we found kindred hearts who shared our excitement and wonder, adding to our sense of awe to be part of something bigger than ourselves.

'Oh, Jesus! Help! Miemie!'

I jumped up and ran out of the house the instant I heard Louis scream. Our friend, Chris, was pinned under the car they were repairing. Only his legs were free. Louis' face was red as he tried to lift the vehicle.

'Pull him… out!'

I grabbed his legs and pulled with all my strength, surprised I managed to move him at all.

'No!' I dropped to my knees, shaking and covered my mouth. Chris' body lay lifeless. His face was like a stranger's, and I immediately recalled the eerie similarity of the grey faces Dad and I had pulled from the river all those years ago. He was dead.

Still puffed from lifting the car, Louis called out to Jesus, and then Chris' chest moved. He breathed!

'Thank you, Jesus! Thank you, Jesus!' We kept saying over and over. The ambulance arrived and took him to hospital. After a few weeks, Chris told the story of how he'd recovered from death, with only healing ribs to show for it, thanks to an awesome, life-giving God.

Chris was our mentor. He and his beautiful wife, Joey, journeyed with us as we moved into home group leadership, hosted prayer nights, presented evangelism courses, and led local outreaches. The day Jesus brought him back to life, we learned that God was not just interested in us when we were inside a church building. He was involved in our everyday lives.

We fell more in love with God as we tasted freedom and understood what grace meant. We were confident we understood—admittedly for the first time—what it meant that God was love. We had been granted the opportunity to experience it all—freedom, love, and grace. Even so, the more we attempted to do for God, the more we felt compelled to do, as we thought it was all conditional. Of course, we believed we had to do our part! We were dedicated to prayer and fasted while living exemplary lives because we did not want to lose what we'd discovered. In the back of our minds, we walked an imaginary thin line between grace and good works. We did the good things because we saw the good results, the miracles, so it was fair to conclude that it was the right thing, that our behaviour kept us in God's good books. We still had much to learn.

THE MALDIVES

Our wedding anniversary was coming up, and after much research, I found some flight specials and booked two weeks' holiday in The Maldives. It was a surprise for Louis, and the first time we would be away from the kids for longer than a weekend.

We discovered the joys of snorkelling, and filled a few photo albums with idyllic pictures of white sandy beaches and palm trees. It was a holiday we would never forget. On the last day, as we headed back to the main island of Malé to catch our flight, my heart raced. I imagined this was what Gideon must have felt like when he put the fleece on the threshing floor and asked God to perform a miracle.

'Okay, God. It is a Saturday.' The sound of the boat's engine drowned out my voice, and it suited me fine. I only needed God to hear me.

'If we get to walk into the government building today and get to see a government official without an appointment, then we'll know it's you.' I looked at the Maldivian people on the boat, I had such compassion for them that it could only have come from God. 'Oh, and he should offer us an island too.'

An hour later, we walked into the government building, and met with a government official who had just happened to pop into the office. After listening to our business proposal, he offered our family some space on an inhabited Maldivian island.

We soared home.

A few months later, we sold our house and packed our lives into a shipping container. We were now missionaries in an Islamic country, based on God's answer to the fleece we put out, and the compassion he placed in our hearts. We knew that we could not come into a Muslin country as missionaries, hence the business venture.

Our new home was an island called Himmafushi, inhabited by around 850 locals (855 with us). The locals spoke Divehi, and very few could speak any English, which meant we depended on hand gestures. The challenges in communication caused a misunderstanding, and we could not access the house we were supposed to rent. Instead, we loaded our furniture off the boat onto the main beach. There was not much we could do until the next day as the capital island, Malé, was an hour's boat ride away, and there were no more trips for the day. So, we stacked our furniture around our mattresses in an attempt to win back a bit of privacy and get some sleep, right there on the beach, with the locals climbing onto our stuff to look at the strange white folks who'd landed on their doorstep. It was not successful.

'Which island you from?' some would ask over and over.

When we responded, 'South Africa', it would be followed with, 'Big island?' Most of them had never seen anything bigger than an island, and had no concept of mountains or rivers. We could walk around Himmafushi in a few minutes, as it was less than a kilometre in length. This was not the idyllic picture one would typically see advertised for holidaymakers.

The following day the problem with our accommodation was sorted out, and we moved into our little home. It was square, with three small rooms and a living space. The outdoor bathroom's wall was constructed of coral, with many peeping holes and no ceiling. Whenever we wanted to take a 'bucket' from the well, as there was no shower, we would need another family member to keep an eye out for any locals scaling the nearby trees to peek at the white-skinned folks.

Being on the equator, the temperature varied by an average of only four degrees Celsius between night and day, and it was constantly humid and stinking hot. When it rained, we would stand in the downpour, thankful for some relief. The ocean remained warm, which meant swimming did not do much to cool us down either. The Maldivian religion required women to be covered up, so in respect for the people, we never appeared in our swimwear on the island. When we wanted to take the kids snorkelling, we would use our small inflatable dinghy and travel to an uninhabited island.

One such day, we pulled our dinghy onto a sandy island and spent the day snorkelling and swimming, mesmerised by the underwater sights and the beauty of the reef. When it was nearly sunset, we packed up to head back home, knowing that we had to be mindful of where the coral reef was so we could avoid it. Unbeknownst to us, while the dinghy had been sitting on the beach, one of the plugs had come undone. It must have worked loose while the boat swayed back and forth in the shallow water.

We headed back, but needed to travel west, which meant the setting sun obstructed our view. By the time we saw the coral reef, it was already too late. One of the engines was damaged and had cut out. My son hopped off to hold the dinghy steady so Louis could inspect the engine, and he accidentally stepped on a sea cucumber which promptly discharged sticky threads all over his foot. Not knowing what it was, we were worried it was something dangerous. We later learned it was harmless, and jetting its internal organs to ensnare its enemies was a defence mechanism.

With the dinghy stationary, and Louis checking the engine, we realised the water was flooding in and then noticed the missing plug. Snorkelling masks doubled as buckets, and we scooped water out with great speed but little success. We panicked when we saw a shark fin heading towards us, and even though we screamed, there was no one near to hear us. The fin reached us, and we laughed. It was part of a coconut tree floating down the current. A local fisherman noticed that we looked a tad frantic and came to our aid. Of course, the entire island stood on the beach, talked loudly and laughed as the fishing boat arrived with us in tow. I could not understand the language, but I imagine they expressed their disbelief in the Westerner's ignorance. We laughed with them and made sure to make our way home with plenty of daylight left next time.

We homeschooled our kids, starting with devotions in the morning. There were countless times when locals from the island would walk into our home, find a seat and watch as we prayed and worshipped. Doors and knocking seemed to have no meaning. Then when devotions were over, they would get up and leave. We thought it strange, but so were many of their other customs, and we learned to quickly move on as the language barrier was no help in discovering answers anyway.

One local, Ahmad, instantly took a liking to our family. He'd invite us to his home for soft drinks or to share a meal, and we quickly learned that their generosity prevailed despite the poor circumstances. Ahmad and his wife had twelve children, his daughters all with names around the variation of Jaada, Vaanda, Naada, and so forth. They lived in poverty like all those on the island, and without meaning to, we became the local clinic. Naturally, anyone with an ailment would ask for help. We offered what we could, as the closest medical service was Malé which meant waiting for a boat, travelling for an hour, followed by unpredictable hours of waiting outside a clinic in the heat. Of course, this quickly depleted our first aid kit. Once, a lady who went into labour sent for me to assist her. How could we not help anyone who asked?

Ahmad worked on a boat, and we were astonished at his craftsmanship using only primitive tools. We would love to stand and watch as he worked.

'You Chrishtans?' Ahmad asked.

'Yes, we are.'

'Pliss, you careful be.'

'Why, Ahmad?'

He shook his head. Curls of shavings formed around his hands and dropped on the sand.

'Uhm, you no say. Tham dead make you when say. You no say, okay?'

'Do you mean that we should not talk about being Christian?'

'Yes, yes, yes. Jail here Chrishtans. Rice food only.'

We knew the island had a jail, as we had passed it many times and seen the men's poor condition through the fence, but this was the first time we'd heard that Christians were locked up there.

Ahmad continued. 'Day says Christian out get, day says shark eat tham. No, no.' He shook his head. 'Day put fish head den put rope on man. Make him walk in water. You no say, okay? Yes?'

We understood.

'Thank you, Ahmad. It is sad to hear what happened to those men, but we cannot deny our faith.'

Ahmad asked us many times over to 'no say', and we could tell he was genuinely concerned. Later, Ahmad shared that if anyone converted to Christianity, they were ostracised and dropped on a deserted island with only a fishing rod. They would starve to death, and we realised that our goal as missionaries would be near impossible if conversions were the aim. So instead, we trusted whatever God wanted us here for, and if it was prayer alone, we would give our best.

Fresh food was in short supply and very expensive, and our canned food was running out, so for several weeks, we lived off the fish we caught (or fish Ahmad gifted us), the flour, which became infected with weevils, eggs, and plenty of rice. When anyone sourced a small watermelon, they would chop it up into slivers and mix it with sugar water to make it go further. We struggled to obtain fresh water, as the well at our home contained sulphur and smelled like rotten eggs. To find variations on what we could make with the basics, we paged through our recipe books and pictures of simple roasted pumpkin left us drooling.

We didn't have much money, only a small amount of savings. We had no income and no missionary support. Despite our better knowledge, we decided to scrape together money to visit a nearby holiday island that hosted a themed buffet dinner each night for holidaymakers. We figured if we could have one good meal with variety, we should be okay for a while. We boarded our dinghy and made sure to stay in the channel carved out of the coral from our island into the open sea towards the neighbouring island. We were hungry for anything Western. We arrived in the last of the daylight, just long enough to view the incredible display of live sharks, stingrays and other hunters of the sea the holiday island had in large pools. When we made our way into the dining area, our hearts sank. The theme for the evening was Maldivian, a buffet with variations of fish and rice dishes, and loads of chilli, of course.

After dinner, we headed back under cover of darkness, with only a flashlight to help us see, hoping that we would not hit coral. Our island had no lights, so we relied on Louis' sense of direction, as the ocean now seemed dark and mysterious, with the cold spray from the waves reminding us of its enormous belly, the same belly holding the large predatory creatures we just saw close-up. We were all relieved when we finally set foot on the island, with no locals on the beach to see us.

Things went downhill, as we had minimal funds left after the business opportunity we hoped to start was blocked at every turn. After four months on the island, things hit an all-time low when we contracted a tropical sickness that caused terrible fever, shivers, body aches and vomiting.

Louis and I walked to a secluded spot on the beach, away from the kids. We wanted to spare them from realising how dire the situation truly was. We kneeled and prayed. We needed a way out. We wanted to stay in God's will but asked him for a way out of this situation, a way back to South Africa. After we prayed, we remained quiet for a moment.

'What did you get?' Louis asked.

'That God honours our obedience, that he will provide a way back.'

'Me too.'

'And… that he would bless us far beyond what we expect.'

'Yeah, the same.'

We got up from our knees, hearts filled with hope and a bit of blind faith. We had no money to pay for plane tickets, no property or anything that would provide an obvious way out. We had each other and the furniture in our home. Soon after, one thing after the other was provided for us, from cheap container transport for our furniture to flights back home. Each time something fell into place, we were relieved and delighted in God's goodness.

I hugged Louis for as long as I could before having to let go. The kids and I were about to board flights to South Africa, and he had to remain behind until the Maldivian government cleared us of all potential financial liabilities associated with the business. Of course, there were none, as we never started, but that was irrelevant.

After we landed in South Africa, I tried to get in touch with Louis. Communication was intolerable, near impossible. Himmafushi had a landline phone in the small government building, and when I rang, which cost a fortune, especially since we did not have enough money to buy food, we would be lucky if someone answered. When they did, I would battle the time delay on the line and the language barrier to ask the other side to call Louis. If they understood me, someone had to run to call him from somewhere on the island, and he would need to make his way to the office. Often, he would never reach the phone, and I would hang up, frustrated at the wasted funds. Finally, when he managed to get to the phone, the sound of each other's voices would cause an instant outburst of tears on both ends. I was relieved that he was alive, and he was missing us more than ever. Phone conversations yielded very little effective communication and caused more trauma, so after a few times of this, we both decided the calls were not worth it.

It was the longest few weeks of our lives. I had no idea if I would see my husband again, and every time I remembered Ahmad's warnings and thought of those poor men who were sent to their deaths, I forced my mind to focus on my kids and to find a way forward for us. I prayed a lot. We all did.

We waited in South Africa with nothing. My nephew mentioned that he had a holiday home in Jeffrey's Bay that he would not rent to holidaymakers as they made a mess of the place. He asked if we would not mind staying there and looking after his house for three months. We felt like kings, living in a luxury holiday home.

My bank account was empty, and we had no vehicle, so I visited the local car dealership and looked at a new car I thought would serve us well, and then walked into the bank branch.

'Could I please see the bank manager?' I asked a teller.

'Sure, for when would you like to make the appointment?' she asked.

'No, I mean, could I speak to the bank manager today?'

'Okay. What would this be in regard to?'

'A car loan.'

'We have someone who deals with that specifically. If you would like to take a seat, he could see you soon.'

'No. This person cannot help me with what I need; I have to speak to the bank manager, please.'

'Uhm, you'll need to wait. He's not available right now.'

'Sure.' I took a seat and waited. Hours later, the manager called me in.

'How can I help you today, Mrs Coetzee?'

'I need a loan for a new car. We've just come from The Maldives, and we have no way to get around. We need this car. I know what you would need from me in this instance; I've done accounting for many years. Unfortunately, I have none of those things to show you. I don't have real estate, no job, no home address, nothing. All I have is one person who owes me a bit of money from the business I sold.' I kept speaking as I wanted the manager to hear everything I had to say before deciding. He shuffled in his seat, but kept listening.

'All I could ask of you is to look at my history with this bank, look at my statements. When I had a loan, I never missed one payment. I don't know how, but I promise you, if you approve this loan, I will pay every cent on time. I promise, I will.' I said the words with conviction and had no idea how I would pay, just that God promised to take care of us. If only the bank would take God's promise as a guarantee.

The bank manager got up and left the office, and I could hear muffled voices from a nearby room. He entered and sat down.

'Listen, I have no idea why I am doing this, as I could lose my job, but I am granting you the loan.'

I bought the car, and miraculously, time after time, the day before the loan was due, there was money in my account. God provided. Although I expected him to provide, each time was as wonderous as the previous.

When the date finally arrived for Louis to be released, I booked his flight and waited. We had no idea if he would be on the flight, but we drove to Port Elizabeth airport anyway. The day before, some money was paid into my account so we could fill up on petrol. We waited for the connection flight from Johannesburg to land and watched through the glass doors as the steps from the plane came down. Our eyes jumped from one person to the next as they filled the doorframe. Finally, when Louis' figure appeared, the staff and doors could not hold us back, and we ran into his embrace on the tarmac, crying and hugging. We were a family again, together, thanking Jesus as we walked to the car.

While we drove home, Louis shared that the Maldivian government returned his passport to him as the release date was nearing, but that the flight booking was before the final business date, which meant the police could arrest him for attempting to leave the country illegally. He stood in line at the airport, terrified but desperate to leave, and as he stepped forward to have his passport checked, a new trainee officer, who had not been issued a uniform yet, was waiting to serve his first customer. The officer was happy to apply his first stamp and handed Louis' passport back to him. Louis swiftly moved towards the plane for boarding, thanking God for another miracle.

Not long after, Louis' previous employer heard the news that we were back in South Africa, and he begged Louis to come back, and offered to pay for our transport and furniture, which was sitting on the dock in a container as we had no funds to clear it. He arranged a home for us, and we started all over again. I picked up my accounting business again, and God blessed us as he'd promised.

Six months later, there were whispers that we were smuggling with diamonds, and we were investigated as they reasoned that it was impossible for anyone to prosper the way we did in such a short time after starting from scratch. I thought it was hilarious and told them to investigate as much as they wanted to. We flourished. God said that he would bless us, we expected it, and he did.

Our lives seemed so full of everything God, that what followed utterly blindsided me.

9

MIRACLES

Over a few weeks, I'd started noticing minor changes in my joints, especially my hands. Simple things became more of a challenge than before—my hands stung as I tried to open jars or grip almost anything. I made the appointment, and my test results returned a positive for arthritis.

I was confused, but not because of the diagnosis. I was in my thirties, and we were in the prime of our lives, in what seemed like the most rewarding place in our spiritual walk with God.

I looked at the diagnosis as an opportunity for God's glory. My healing would mean a living testimony that could help show others the way, lead them to salvation. I lifted my chin, asked for prayer at church, prayed myself, fasted, and attended healing services. I was optimistic, as I could see the bigger picture.

Days turned into weeks as one unanswered prayer for healing followed another.

Especially on our way to prayer meetings, my mind would loop through the same questions. If God is the healer, and he does heal, why not me? Why does sickness exist, and why did I get sick? Did I do something wrong? It must be me. God does not make mistakes, so it must be my fault.

At the meeting, I would place a lot of hope in the person who prayed for me because God used them to heal. Then, on multiple occasions, after prayer, I would be healed. The pain would be gone, and my fingers were mine again. During these times, blissful joy flooded me, wrapped in intense gratefulness that the God of the universe would show me such kindness and grace that he would spend time taking away my sickness. There were always tears, and my heart would quietly and humbly spill over with thankfulness while my mind would constantly dissect everything I knew—measure what happened against my beliefs. Every time I would be cautious not to get on the wrong side of whatever caused this sickness. It was tough, as I could not identify the cause.

At most, a couple of weeks is all I had before the pain would return and the process would start all over. And then I would hear of someone else who prayed for the sick, or I would hear of a new healing-related method, and that was my new hope for a while until I got healed and then ill again. And the seesaw continued.

When ministering to others, I'd trained myself to ignore the doubts and focus on the miracles rather than lack of miracles. However, I could no longer ignore the growing internal whirlwind as my own incessant questions remained unanswered. Some of the most dedicated Christians I knew continually prayed for their sick child. Their child remained unwell. They persevered in prayer and fasting—still, no healing. That was one of many examples in our circle of influence. My heart would break for them, and usually, I would force myself to see the goodness of God in the situation, dismiss the reason for the lack of a miracle to either God's plan for them to somehow grow through the situation or them doing something wrong, but I could do so no longer.

My internal struggle, hidden from the world, shaped my view of God and myself. If this arthritis was not there for God to heal so that he could be glorified through the healing, what was it for? It did not fit. This was not supposed to happen to me. Not with me, not with us. How was

I supposed to pray for the sick when I was ill myself? It felt like a death sentence each time the pain returned. If I could not pray for the sick, and I could not deliver a testimony that could lead someone to salvation, what good was I?

I was letting God down.

'Why did I not get healed?' I felt a little arrogant asking the pastor who'd prayed for me, but I needed an answer. If anyone knew, it would be him. He was renowned for healing miracles.

'God did all he could. I laid hands and prayed. Now it is up to you. If you are not healed, it is because you left a door open for the devil, and it usually stems from resentment.'

If the pastor, God's instrument for healing, did all he could, then the problem was me. I knew it was me. Without delay, I self-examined every aspect of my life, analysed each of my relationships to see where the resentment was in my heart. I prayed and fasted and was careful not to allow any bitterness into my life. Despite taking utter care of my spiritual life, the healing and sickness cycle continued for the next two decades, except for one Sunday in 1997.

Had you asked me to describe what I felt that Sunday morning, I would have hesitated and probably not told you anything. It was wonderful, the unfamiliar feeling that I wanted to treasure. So, I was scared to define it, to box it with words. The intensity and novelty of what I sensed had already announced that I could anticipate something different, something good. As usual, we got ready for church, and I kept to myself, my attention focused on an awareness of floating that seemed to carry me as I walked. At church, it was as if I could not remain seated in my chair. Everything of that day seemed a bit lighter, a bit easier. A visiting pastor was preaching for this Sunday's service, and I felt self-conscious as he kneeled and took my hand and said the strangest thing, 'I wish I had what you have.'

I shook my head, as I wished no attention and could not make much sense of any of it. We left for home after the service, and I knew I was healed. It was strange, as it did not match any of our previous miracle experiences. No one prayed for me—I did not ask. My focus was on the enjoyment of the floating feeling. The arthritis was just gone! I did not pray beforehand or fast. It was out of sorts. I held my breath and waited for the arthritis to return after a couple of weeks, as per usual. After almost three years went by without any sign of joint pain, I was cautiously optimistic that it was permanently gone. I kept thanking Jesus for the miracle, while constantly scanning over my relationships to ensure that I would not allow any resentment into my life. I was confused yet grateful. Whatever I did (or did not do) kept the sickness at bay. When the pain slowly crept back into my joints, I wanted to deny it at first, but daily tasks became a battle again. It got worse, and I knew it.

From this point forward, my focus was to obtain healing. I meditated, prayed, fasted, tried to rid my heart of any resentment, dissected my life for any possible doors I might have left open, attended multiple repentance sessions where I tried to rid myself of anything known and unknown that could have caused the illness. I searched for years for the next 'new' thing that God was doing, moving from one religious method to the next. There was little I did not pursue or try.

Despite my struggle with arthritis, our lives had no shortage of sick and needy people and with that came an abundance of healings and wonders.

Just outside our town, Louis Trichardt, lived a small community of coloured people we reached out to after church on Sundays. They were known as the *Buisdorpers*, the name derived from *Buis,* the family last name, and *dorpers*, referring to a small township. The political climate in South Africa meant these folks belonged nowhere. They were not black, nor were they white. They were known as brown people, overlooked and misunderstood.

We would bring a picnic lunch and the families added to the table whatever they could, meaning Sunday lunch was a potluck feast. White folks like us were not seen near the Buisdorpers, as they were viewed as subordinate outcasts. So when we sat down and had lunch with them, we were not just sharing the Gospel, but showing them that someone cared, that they were loved. These folks were incredibly poor, and many needs stretched from healing to finances. As they saw our acceptance of them and that we genuinely cared, they brought specific prayer requests, and God was faithful to heal and provide time and time again.

Overjoyed, our day-to-day lives were propelled by the never-ending zeal to show others how wonderful life could be, to lead them to salvation, and we opened our home to others in our community who needed help.

A social worker from our church community approached us one morning after the service.

'Just wondering if you might be able to help. This week, I found a man, probably in his forties, who lives in his car next to the dam. He has nowhere else to go. He, uhm, tried to commit suicide. The poor guy is in such a miserable headspace right now, admittedly drunk most of the time, but I just know… if he attempts suicide again, he will be successful.'

His disheartening situation became clear later that day when he limped into our living room, sat his crutches aside and told us what happened.

'I went boating on the dam, had too much to drink and when I fell into the water by accident, the propeller chopped into my foot.' He looked at his foot and sighed deeply. 'It's mutilated, and there is nothing the doctors can do for me. The worst thing is the never-ending pain. I can't step on my foot at all. I don't sleep, and I know I drink too much.'

We listened as he told us his wife had kicked him out, and his kids wanted nothing to do with him. He admitted to knowing that he was like a different person when he was drunk. When he broke into tears and told us that he had nothing to live for, our hearts ached for him.

'There is hope. You're welcome to stay with us.'

He was grateful and joined the two other guys who had been living with us since being released from jail and having nowhere else to go.

Church on a Sunday was a wonderful time of connection with the larger community, but cell group was where we thrived. The smaller intimate setting on a Friday evening with people we could share life with, provided the platform for specific prayer requests, sharing of the Word of God and answering questions on the practical side of living as a Christian.

One of our favourite things to do was place a chair in the middle of the room, and anyone who needed prayer could sit in it. We would all lay hands, pray and agree. The number of answered prayers were incredible and we could barely wait for the next meeting to share all the testimonies. It became one celebration after the next, and our cell group grew exponentially as more and more people joined. The pastor said the group was becoming too big, that we had to split into smaller cells, but no one wanted to leave; it was too exciting to see what God was doing.

It was during this time that the man with the mangled foot lived with us. On the first Friday evening, we invited him to sit in the chair in the middle of our group, everyone brimming with excitement and hopeful anticipation to pray for someone else.

'Nah. I don't want to,' he protested.

'Come on, this is great, you just get to sit and relax, and we pray.' One of the cell members tried to encourage him.

'No, nothing is going to change. My foot won't change. It will just be further disappointment; I'd rather not.'

'Well, if you don't want to believe, that is fine. We'll believe for you!'

He sat in the chair anyway, and we all got to pray for him. He got up, shook his head and retired for the evening, and slept for the first night in a long time.

Early the following day, we heard screaming and shouting and found this man, as well as the two other blokes in our living room, dancing and jumping like kids in their pyjamas.

This man screamed, 'I'm healed! My foot is healed! Look, I can step on it!'

We all cried and laughed and shouted, praising Jesus for the miracle. His entire countenance changed, and people who had known him before did not recognise him. He looked younger, filled with light and joy, and the drinking ceased. He said that God touched him and changed him.

After the change, I went to see his wife, told her about the miracle and how different he now was. She wanted to know nothing about it, said that he could not change, that she feared him and would never take him back. After much back-and-forth, she reluctantly agreed to join us with him during a Christian singer-songwriter performance one evening. The public space provided her with some security, and she was free to leave any time. I could sense her resistance and understood the reluctance to believe that he was a new man, but we all hoped that she would see it as plain and clear as everyone else did.

The entire cell group went along on the next date, a casual braai or barbeque, expectant and holding our breaths. I spoke to her beforehand, saying that I would remain by her side and if she felt pressured or threatened in any way, she did not have to say anything but simply look at me, and I would know and walk out with her. She agreed. He and his wife were seated next to each other, and at one point, one of the cell group members pumped me in the ribs and whispered, 'Look, they're holding hands!'

I leaned over and smiled. They looked like a young couple in love, and later that day, she rested her head on his shoulder. He shone like the sun with tears in his eyes, and we witnessed God restore a marriage. She invited him back home, and he could not pack his bags fast enough.

After Nelson Mandela became president in 1994, affirmative action was introduced, which meant if you were white, work opportunities were scarce, and almost non-existent for white males. Another family that crossed our path during this time lived in extreme poverty. They were one of many families who could not find jobs because of their skin colour, and they were further disadvantaged because they had no formal education and their adult son had a mental disability. With no government support, the husband fished for food; otherwise, they had maize or potatoes and cabbage to eat. They had no stove, so the lady cooked on a *konka*—a large drum with perforated sides, its belly filled with coals, used for outdoors cooking. Despite their circumstances, we could see the beauty in their hearts. These people slept on mattresses on the floor, yet always seemed to have space for anyone without a place to stay. It seemed that there were always extra people, and they regularly shared what little food they had.

We were delighted when the adult son set his reluctance aside and sat in the chair in the centre of our cell group on Friday evening. Louis explained that God would give us the desires of our heart, that we just had to ask.

'I'd like a job,' he said.

'Okay. But what kind of job? You have to be specific.' Louis said.

'Uhm. I'd like a paint job. The one where you paint cars.' We prayed, not ignorant of the improbability of his situation.

His mum sat down next. 'If I could have a small stove, I'd be so grateful.'

Again, we prayed.

On Sunday at church, someone mentioned that they were renovating their kitchen and wondered if anyone needed a stove. On Tuesday, we took a very fancy stove to this lady, and as we carried it into her yard, she fell to her knees in the dust and thanked Jesus. That same week the son landed a job as a vehicle painter.

These and other miracles, including the healing of schizophrenia, diabetes and ulcers, amongst others, consumed our lives with everything God, and it was terrific! We loved our leadership journey.

Nothing was impossible for God!

Or so it seemed. All around me, miracles were unfolding, yet I continued to struggle with arthritis.

A challenge with impossible odds energised me. I thrived on seeing these challenges overcome and helping a client out of a desperate situation. Keeping them in the black was what made my accounting business personal. It was not just numbers on a sheet; it was people, their livelihood and their future.

My business was bursting at the seams, yet I could not send away the couple who walked into my office. A medical doctor and his wife explained that their private practice was to undergo sequestration, a process by which their property and assets would be taken over by a liquidator and sold off to pay creditors. They asked me for help to see the process through. I felt heartbroken for them, as they looked like they had given up, and this was a necessary last step in a long and heavy journey.

'We are almost two years behind in office rent. Our expenses are overwhelming. The company who owns the complex where our offices are is also our landlord.' The doctor produced a sheet with red printed letters from his file. 'This is the final notice.'

I looked at it for a second. 'Are you aware that going through with sequestration, you are, for all intents and purposes, permanently closing down any future options for private practice?' Again, I looked at the doctor, 'Your only choice after this would be a doctor in the army or working as a hospital employee.'

'That is not what I want, but we see no other way out.'

I took a deep breath and looked them in the eyes. 'Listen, you're so deep in trouble in any case, allow me to try a few things? I'll write to your landlord and ask for an extension and present them with a payment plan. You have income, and where there is income, there is always a way.'

They shook their heads, and I could sense how disheartened they were when the doctor spoke again, 'There really is nothing else that anyone can do. You'll see when you open the books; it is impossible.'

'You have nothing to lose. Just give me a chance.'

They agreed, albeit reluctantly, but that was all I needed.

I set to work, drafted a budget and called the doctor the next day. 'I have a plan, but you need to know if you do not stick to the budget, you should look for another accountant.'

'So, we're not going through with sequestration?' I could hear the doubt in his voice.

'Not if the landlord agrees to the plan.'

After a few weeks of extension, the landlord issued my client with notice of legal action, and I immediately contacted the company's legal department to arrange a meeting in person. If they could meet the doctor, see the person, they might not be so quick to ruin his life. They agreed, though my client thought it was a waste of time.

The travel to the company's offices took a few hours, and I used the opportunity.

'I know you don't believe in God, doctor, but I do, and I need to ask you something.'

The doctor frowned slightly. 'Okay?'

'You know as well as I do, that we cannot turn this situation around. I believe with all my heart that God will lead us in this. He can change all this for the better. So, I am going to pray before we walk into that meeting, and I need you to agree with me. Can you do that?'

He nodded and I started to pray.

'Father God, thank you for your grace. Thank you that you will lead us, that nothing is impossible for you, that you will turn the situation around. Amen.'

We got out of the car, and my heart pounded in my chest. There in the parking area stood a white Mercedes I would recognise anywhere. The registration belonged to a well-renowned lawyer from our region. She had a reputation for spotting loopholes, and a fierceness and confidence which girded her incredible skills and success rate. This lawyer was also married to a judge. I had no idea she would be at the meeting. Frankly, I had no idea who would attend at all, but the lawyer's presence punctuated the seriousness of our predicament. My stomach felt like it had been left behind as we took the elevator, but despite my insides shaking, I kept up a brave face for my client. We entered the luxurious conference room, and the doctor staggered backwards as fourteen faces on the opposite side of the table met the two of us. We took our seats, and the legal team piled papers in the middle of the table as they verbalised the facts of the case. When the lawyer finished, she leaned back and crossed her arms.

'Okay,' I said with as much confidence as I could muster. 'While you are presenting the facts, allow me to present a few as well. Are you aware of the email correspondence from my client to you regarding the noise level in the complex next door, which you also own? Do you know that two examination rooms have air conditioners out of order which makes those rooms intolerably hot in summer and therefore unusable to my client?'

The directors looked at the legal team and I continued. 'This qualifies for a breach in contract as you did not provide the facility as agreed. What if my client misdiagnosed a patient because of the noise, especially given that most of his patients are non-English speaking and communication is challenging? I wonder what a judge would think of that?'

The lawyer asked to see the contract, flicked through it, then looked at the company directors, and shook her head.

That was my indicator, 'Okay, could you write off half of the rent debt, and we will present you with a payment plan for the remainder?' So, with that, I handed over the payment plan. 'I promise you we will be true to this plan.'

I held my breath. It was an incredible amount of money we were asking the company to simply write off.

The lawyer spoke. 'I know this lady. If she says she will take care of this, she will.'

We shook hands, and I heard my client breathe for the first time. The elevator doors barely closed when he spoke, 'You're a wonderful person!'

'No. You're making a big mistake. It is not me. It is the God I serve who is wonderful; he turned this around for you.' We took each others' hands and thanked Jesus.

That day changed my client's life as he started to seek Jesus. He believed! His medical practice started to thrive.

Many cases like this left me entirely thankful that my Father cared for the hearts of people, my clients. There was often no logical way out. When things turned around for the better, I knew it was not me, but God, and I would feel the familiar warmth of gratefulness because of his grace.

BLIND FAITH IN A
NEW COUNTRY

My accounting business did well, as I focused on a few larger clients where we lived in Louis Trichardt, allowing me to work from home most days. My clients, such as Thompson Motors and Mountain View Hotel, were not just companies I worked for. They were people I cared about, and my work reflected such as I strived to give them the best service possible. The owners of the companies became close family friends and were dear to me.

With the changes in South Africa in the 1990's, crime spiked and multiple layers of security were essential for our safety. We fitted our home with barbed wire, electrical fencing and automated gates. Windows already had permanent burglar bars. We installed an alarm system supported by armed response units, with a panic button under my desk should I need it. The living area was separate from the bedrooms, and the hallway was divided by an internal security gate that would be locked before we retired for the night. I never went anywhere without my 9mm hand pistol strapped to my body, or if my outfit did not allow for this, I kept it in my handbag. It was unwise and unsafe to do otherwise.

It may sound like overkill, but it was not uncommon. Despite this, neighbours down our street were brutally murdered. Then our close friends, the owners of Mountain View Hotel, were killed. Finally, when my brother was attacked and left for dead, it was too close to home. We wanted to find somewhere for our kids to have a future, a life.

While holidaying in America and Europe, we not only looked through tourist eyes, but also with a view to possible immigration. None of these places felt right. Some of our friends also looked at other options, and we started considering Australia as a potential future home. I noticed that accountants were on the immigration shortlist, which meant Australia had a shortage of accountants, significantly increasing the chances of a visa approval with me as the primary applicant.

I decided I could complete the visa application myself and deal with the immigration process. We did not need an immigration agent; besides, I did not have the patience to wait on someone else to get things done for me, and in the process, I would save thousands. The folders of paperwork we were required to complete were immense, but we pushed on and deep inside, I understood what my ancestors must have felt when they searched for a new place for them and their children. They fled from persecution and made their way to South Africa all those years ago. This was not the first time Louis and I started over, not the first generation compelled to look for a future for their kids.

I applied for multiple accountant positions advertised in Australia and received no response. After some time, I realised I needed to get on a plane and apply from Australia if I wanted to land a job. So, on a visitor's visa, I booked my ticket, as did my friend. By this time, the older two of our children were adults and our youngest a teenager. My friend and I booked the same flight. We would go together to look for work, and then our families would follow. That was the plan.

On the 11th of November 2004, we said goodbye to our families and made our way through airport security to the terminal. I knew the separation would be challenging, as Louis and I had not been apart this long before. My return ticket was in a month. When the wheels of the plane lifted, my friend was still sobbing.

'I'm not coming back.' I wanted to get her focus off the crying and onto Australia and finding a new life for our families. I could not help but talk about the burning expectation in my gut.

'What do you mean?' She wiped her cheeks.

'I just know—I'm never coming back to South Africa again.'

'But how can you say that?'

'I just know that the Lord will provide for me, that he will make a path for me.'

'But you need to come back and pack and—'

'Louis is grown up enough to manage that. I'm going to open up a new road for us; he could close up the old one.'

We landed in Sydney, found a hotel and decided to take a walk outside to explore Australia. We passed a lady standing at her front gate and asked for directions to a café so we could buy some soft drinks. She invited us in and served us drinks. I could not believe the hospitality, opposite to our lives in South Africa, where we had to lock ourselves up to stay safe. Inviting strangers into your home? Never!

Over the next few weeks, I applied for every accounting position advertised. My friend went on to Brisbane, as she had friends there. Back in South Africa, our home sold, and Louis had to move out within the month, so he packed our furniture into a shipping container and sent it to Australia. He stayed with family, and we would Skype each day with an update. Due to the time difference, I'd have to wait until at least 2 pm Australian time to ring, so that it would be 6 am in South Africa and Louis would be able to take my call. Waiting was torture.

'Can't believe it's been over three weeks! I miss you terribly. Have you heard anything back from the accounting positions?'

'Nothing yet, but I'm thinking of heading to Queensland this weekend.'

'Are you going to stay with Amarinda?'

'Yes, I spoke to her this morning. Can you believe it's been eight years since they moved to Australia? She mentioned there is less work in Queensland than here, but I'm not getting any responses here in New South Wales, so I must be in the wrong place. God must have other plans.'

'Okay, so are you going to extend your return flight date then?'

'I don't think so.'

It was hard for Louis and me to be apart, even more complex as our future did not seem certain. We had limited cash, and the exchange rate was around ten Rands for an Australian dollar, which meant anything Australian was expensive, very expensive. A few days before my return flight was due; tensions were exceptionally high.

'Come back, Miemie. Just leave everything and we can start over again somewhere else, even if we live in the desert, as long as we can be together again. I'm lost without you.'

'I'm not coming back. I know that God will make a way somehow.'

That night I sat on my bed and opened the red folder with all my paperwork. In the front, I had handwritten a scripture verse from Isaiah that I had made my own: 'See, I am doing a new thing! Now it springs up; do you not perceive it? I am making a way in the wilderness and streams in the wasteland' (Isa. 43:19 NIV).

That was *my* promise. If God could make a way in the wilderness, he could easily make way for me. I trusted him unequivocally, knew that he would look after us, though I did not know how. It was my job to find the way he made. I could feel Louis' pain, and understood where he was coming from. Our lives were uprooted, and there was nothing sure in sight. We just had each other, and there was an ocean between us. I flipped through the paperwork and pulled my return flight ticket from its sleeve. It would expire in two days. I stared at it for a moment and then tore the ticket in half. I was not going to let the ticket be a temptation. I would take God at his word. There was no *or*, or *but*, or *if*.

I arrived at Amarinda's place in Fernvale, Queensland on the Sunday, and we picked up where we'd left off. It was as if no time had passed, that there had never been distance between us. It was so wonderful to see her again. Amarinda is my second eldest brother's firstborn. The moment I first saw her, my six-year-old heart believed she was my baby, and we were inseparable. I bathed and fed her, put her to sleep, and took care of her the way a mother would. Even throughout our primary school years together, the special mother-sister bond we had was unique. That bond has remained throughout our lives.

I bought the Sunday newspaper and immediately started applications for accounting positions. As I took my paperwork out and put it on the table, Amarinda shrieked.

'Miemie, what are you doing with your resume and reference letters?'

'What do you mean?'

'You're not meant to carry them in your suitcase with a visitor's visa! If you got caught, they would have sent you straight back to South Africa.'

I honestly did not know that. No-one checked my bag. I started to see God's hand making a way for me. With all the challenges I faced, God's goodness was evident, and I believed without reason, convinced that I had to take the step over the edge of the boat, like Peter and keep my eyes on Jesus.

On Monday I sent in forty job applications. I also met Amarinda's neighbour who told me that she worked at an accounting firm, and they were looking for an accountant. This was no coincidence. I saw God's hand at work when I was appointed the position, and my faith surged. Having secured a job, I immediately applied for a permanent visa, as a lady from immigration had advised I could do so. A few weeks later, I received a phone call from the immigration offices.

'You cannot apply for a permanent visa while on a visitor's visa.'

'Why not?'

'Because visitor's visas have a 'no further stay' condition. It's in your passport.'

With the officer on the line, I grabbed my passport and checked the visa. 'No, it's not in mine.'

'It should be there.'

I decided to go to Brisbane and take my passport to the immigration offices. They checked. The condition was not part of my visitor visa. They were baffled. I tried not to grin, but my heart was pounding with gratefulness. Strange? Nope. I took the absence of the standard condition as another sign of God's hand at work. I believed that I belonged in Australia. I was delighted that my permanent visa would be processed, that I did not have to leave the country to re-apply. Besides, we were short on funds, and I'd ripped up my plane ticket.

Not long after, I received an email from immigration. They had declined my permanent visa.

At this point, I could have given up and gone back to South Africa. Nothing worked out. We were out of funds, we were separated, it has been too long. But why would God bring me this far only to drop me now?

I went to Brisbane again to see the officer who'd declined my visa. I wanted to know why this had happened after being advised by an officer from immigration that I could apply. He told me that I first had to apply for a 457 temporary visa and stay on that visa for at least three months before applying for a permanent visa. There was no point in pondering the error. I was going to fix it and make sure there were no other mistakes and get the next visa application in. I immediately filled out the paperwork and paid the application fee. And then I waited.

I rented a small house in Rosewood, close to the accounting firm. The only furniture I had was a mattress that Amarinda had given me. Whoever said patience is a virtue must not have shared my temperament. I wanted things done yesterday. I had nothing to do but wait. And so I spent endless hours walking and praying. Hours of talking to God about the same thing over and over again in many different ways. That he would make a way, for his guidance and the right people at the right place, for good timing—that was a big one, also that the visa would be approved. After many kilometres of walking, my feet started to ache more than usual. I suspected it had something to do with arthritis, but brushed it off as my focus was on the end goal—on my family having a better life in Australia and my God who can make a way in the wilderness. I dared not get distracted or focus on what was usual in the visa process because I needed the extraordinary, and I believed with all my heart. I refused to trust my circumstances or the standard expectations. Deep inside, I was convinced that the events had to change to line up with what I believed.

And then, a few weeks later, after what felt like an eternity, an email from immigration landed in my inbox. My hand shook, and my heart felt as if it would pound through my throat as I clicked on the subject line. I read the first line of the email, instantly became lightheaded, and sobbed. I dropped to my knees and then laughed and cried simultaneously. 'Thank you, Lord Jesus. Thank you for your goodness. Oh, thank you!' It was an early morning in March, and the clock would not move fast enough that day. I wanted it to be 2 o'clock so I could call Louis and tell him the fantastic news, let him know that I had booked his flight. I felt like I was running on water.

A condition of the 457 visa was the completion of Australian tax law, as it was different to South African tax. I grew up with Afrikaans as my first language, and my studies, business, and daily life were Afrikaans, so I rarely needed to correspond in English. I always messed up the tenses, and barely speaking English did nothing for improving my skills. Could I pass a subject in English? I had to if we wanted a future in Australia, so I persuaded myself that it was possible. I could do it!

Australia was our future, and that meant English was my new language. I tripped over words, and conversing was exhausting as I grappled with how to string English words together so I would make sense. I could not ask if the person spoke Afrikaans like in South Africa—I simply had to adjust. And quickly. But then I found out that English is not English in Australia, or at least not as I expected.

My first few experiences with Australians made me fall in love with the friendly people, but I could not understand much of what they were saying, and my accent was thick, so they did not always understand me either. The words coming from their lips were English, but on top of the Aussie accent, the meaning was completely different. If I was invited for *tea*, it was not a cup of tea with biscuits; it was a meal. And *barbie*? Not a doll, but a barbecue or *braai* in my reference.

I found out that greeting does not work the same as the South African way either. In Australia, folks would say, 'G'day, how are ya?' and then continue with their business, where I would automatically rattle off the remainder of the phrase, 'Fine thank you, and how are you?' They would look up almost in surprise and say, 'Oh, I'm fine too. Thanks for asking,' as if asking how they were in response was odd and unexpected. I learned that asking how someone was doing did not need a reply; it was the actual greeting.

I made sure to highlight the date in my diary, exactly three months since the 457 temporary visa was approved. I took the day off work and went to the immigration offices in Brisbane to submit my permanent visa. I was 44, and one of the visa conditions required a successful applicant to be under 45 years of age. Amarinda warned me that no visa is approved in such a short time and that I should consider other options. It generally took many months, even years. I did not want to hear any of it, just replied, 'You'll see,' and kept praying, kept believing that God would make a way, again. It had to work out somehow, there was no alternative in my mind. In June, three days before my 45th birthday, the permanent visa was approved.

I jumped for joy and danced. Never would we be sent back to South Africa; Australia was our home now. We were permanent residents. We could not read the word 'indefinite' stamped in our passports enough times. Each time either Louis or I read it, we would laugh with happiness. We celebrated God's goodness that evening with a glass of wine, a nice dinner and hearts overflowing with gratefulness.

We loved Australia. We adored the people and the freedom to walk down the street and not to have to be on guard against mugging or worse. We felt safe. Small things like the water fountains and clean public toilets, the reliable public transport and the beautiful towns left us astounded and grateful to be part of this gorgeous country.

The day we finally became Australian citizens was like reaching the mountain summit. We proudly displayed our Australian flag and celebrated with a BBQ with our Aussie friends. We watched the Australian movie 'The Castle' and screamed laughing as we caught on to the once strange humour. We were fluent, or mostly fluent, in Aussie slang and used words like cozzie, arvo, hubby and Maccas.

Despite many years of English practice, my accent remains, and I would sometimes be engrossed in a task and forget to translate my thoughts. Once, the receptionist at the office brought me a client file, and I thanked her in Afrikaans without thinking.

'Baie dankie.'

'Buy a donkey!' she repeated with indignation.

I had to quickly explain that meant 'thank you very much' and I was not instructing her to buy a donkey. We had a good laugh, and despite my best efforts, I still respond in Afrikaans some days when deep in thought or tired.

I was thrilled when Louise moved to Australia a short time after and Christo followed some years later. We now had all our kids permanently living in Australia. Other family and friends joined us over time, and Louis and I were blessed to become grandparents many times over. Our grandkids are true Aussies, born and bred here. We speak to them in Afrikaans, and they often reply in English, and should they speak Afrikaans, it is with an adorable Aussie accent.

After seeing more of Australia, we decided to buy a rural property in the Gympie region in 2009. At the time, I felt blessed to be working remotely from my home office as the senior accountant for a company. Office visits were only necessary once a month unless something urgent popped up.

When I experienced a sudden flare up and swelling in my hands and feet, it became too painful to walk, and I decided to see a doctor. The diagnosis upgraded my arthritis to rheumatoid arthritis and Hashimoto's disease—both autoimmune diseases. My body's immune system was attacking my tissue and joints, which explained the painful swelling and inflammation. Over time, the inflammation caused bone erosion and my finger joints disformed, leaving unsightly lumps. The doctor prescribed weekly doses of Methotrexate to slow my immune system, as well as strong painkillers. I took the Methotrexate, but avoided the painkillers whenever possible and only opted for these when the pain became intolerable. I never liked taking medication.

The doctors told me there was no cure for what I had. I could not believe that. Over the next eight years, I continued my search for healing. On top of everything I had done up to this point, I engaged in Heavenly courts, stepped in and out of heaven, took communion three times a day, recited declarations, delved into family history, performed DNA cleansing, and even repented for the sins of previous generations—nothing worked. I repeated methods and steps nevertheless, as that was all I knew how to do. There had to be an answer somewhere.

THE DAY I DIED

On the 24th of November 2017, the day I died, the morning started in the conventional way. I was up before the alarm, before the sun, as the first bird welcomed the day with its song. As always, coffee was a priority. I struggled to grip the lid of the milk container. Hundreds of needles pierced through my fingers. Early mornings were the worst. My lips pinched, and my jaw tightened as I pushed through the pain. Finally, the lid surrendered, and my face softened. I love life, do not get me wrong, but I despise the pain, the suffering that rheumatoid arthritis brought— limiting my movements, hindering any efficiency, stalling my work, sabotaging my life. Farm work did not hit 'pause' just because I moved slower. The work piled up.

I took a sip of coffee and decided to skip the pain medication. Instead, I pulled my grey gloves on, slowly, meticulously, one finger at a time. Armed with my gloves and coffee, I walked to my home office and pressed the start button on the computer. I had an hour or so to myself before Louis was up and needed me, so I set to work balancing the turnover and cash accounts for the company I worked for. The gloves' pressure brought enough relief for me to type at a reasonable pace, though nothing like the breakneck speed I could muster in my younger days. In times like these, I felt grateful that I could work from home.

The clacking of the keys should have disguised the tightness in my belly that thrust the tears up through my chest, my throat, and out through my eyes. It did a poor job. In a sweeping gesture, I wiped the tears from my cheeks and sneered. I felt that notorious question swirling in my mind. *Why? Why all this suffering? Why me?* Maybe this time, I will figure it out. And the stage was set, yet again, for the futile debate that was so familiar to me. I recalled John 10:10 stating we should have life and that in abundance. *So how come I do not have that life?* As evidence, I paraded the excessive list of things I'd attempted in order to achieve this abundant life, this freedom from sickness: the flights to well-known healer meetings; the prayers—both begging and declaring; the stepping in and out of Heaven; the 'new' spiritual experiences turned into a method to be followed precisely; the hours, days, weeks of end-to-end lectures and talks (because the answer must be in the next one). My eyes caught the pages of boldly printed declarations all over my office wall—the ritual recital, declaring each morning and evening and sometimes whenever I saw them. It all felt wearisome, all unsuccessful in freeing me from this debilitating pain.

The debate in my mind presented the opposition, *'If I had faith'.* A mixture of disbelief and fury surfaced as I recalled the moment I read the document yet another well-known healer sent after he'd prayed for me, and I'd asked again about not getting any better.

'Even if you don't see any change, do not say you are not healed. Live as if you are.' It felt like a wet blanket of despair covered me when I read those words. I remember staring at my hands with the protruding lumps near each joint, and I burst into tears. I could barely bend my fingers. Even though it was not said like that, or probably not meant like that, I felt judged. I felt the flaw was me. *I had faith!* I have believed for many years now. I have not accepted the sickness, and I know that God is our healer. As I have been taught, I know that God does not bring disease, but why does he not take mine away? I shook my head, thinking of everything I had dedicated my life to—mission work, outreaches, church. What about all the great moments—the miracles, the healed people as we ministered? *Is it just not for me then? Others could get healing, but not me? Why me?*

Louis walked in and kissed me. 'Good morning, *Ounooi.*'

I looked up and smiled at his term of endearment for me and buried the internal debate in an instant.

'Good morning. Did you sleep well?'

He looked at me while leaning against the desk. 'You okay?'

I wanted to scream, *No! How am I supposed to make sense of all this?* Instead, I nodded, 'Yeah, of course.'

'How about another coffee?' he motioned in the direction of the empty coffee mug on the desk.

'That would be great.' I got up and followed him to the kitchen.

'It would be fantastic if we could make some progress on the dam today.' He took two mugs from the cupboard. 'Are you able to help me clear some trees this morning?'

'Yeah, sure. It is Friday after all, and I finished what I needed for the office.' I rubbed my fingers and through the window, admired the blend of red and yellow as the sun lifted over the mountain. I loved the view from our living area overlooking the valley.

'Coffee.' Louis placed the mug in my hands, and we sat down to savour a few minutes of calm before the workday started.

A restlessness tugged at my insides, and I tried to shrug it off as I got dressed slowly, carefully, to minimise pain. It was mid-summer, and we preferred to get work done early mornings when the air was still cool.

I decided it would be better to assist Louis, who was moving the fallen trees from the field with the large tractor, than work on my own. As I steered the small tractor, nervous tension kept flaring up at the slightest slip of the wheels. It was odd. I do not consider myself an anxious person, but it had been like that all morning. What was wrong with me? I steered my tractor to the side of the road and switched the engine off. I took my mobile out of my pocket and sat it on the front of the tractor. At least I would not be on a machine, and with less chance of something bad happening, my nerves could stop harassing me! I grabbed the tie-down straps I needed for the tree clearing and hung them around my neck instead of burdening my hands with the weight.

Mud greeted my shoes in squelchy retaliation as it dispersed with every step. Fallen trees with exposed roots lay scattered across the field, evidence of the excavator's completed work. There was still a lot to be done before this uneven area would become a dam. Plenty of rain allowed nature to respond in a gorgeous display of green, and the mud reminded me to take the unpleasant with the delightful—it was all part of farm life. It was hard work, but I still found joy in nature and seeing a dream come to life.

The large tractor's sound filled the morning air as Louis hauled another tree from the valley to the other side where the outer edges of the dam wall would be. Without help, Louis had to steer the tractor backwards up a steep slope towards the fallen trees, get off, fasten a tie-down strap around a tree, get back on the tractor and haul it forwards and downhill to where the trees were piled. I negotiated my way on foot across the field towards him, zigzagging around trees and uneven earth. I could feel Louis' appreciation as I hooked a strap around the end of a massive tree, just beyond the large lateral roots that poked to the side, while he reversed the tractor uphill towards me. As the tractor paused to a low hum, I attached the strap to the hook on the tractor's back. The engine kicked into work mode again, ready to pull the tree down the valley, roots first. I quickly moved at a ninety-degree angle away from the tree. And then my minds' eye saw a horrific scene, like a premonition.

The tree jerked to life when the tractor moved forward and pulled it downhill. Instead of following the tractor, it rolled over sideways. As if alive, a defiant root speared the ground. The rest of the tree became airborne, swung like a crane and whiplashed in my direction.

Surely what I thought I saw was not happening? I turned to look back.

My heart sank.

I had an overwhelming urge to run. The mud and holes and uphill terrain fought harder than my legs could carry me. It was too late. The force of the impact flung me through the air, and I heard the sickening sound of cracking bones. I hit the ground and immediately knew my injuries were significant.

'Jesus!' My desperate call was shadowed by the eeriest sounds escaping my lips. I knew my lung was punctured. I tried to stop the sounds, but had no control over them. Pain, unlike anything I had ever experienced in my 58 years of living, throbbed through my body. My left arm was awkwardly tucked into my torso. My chest felt like it was on fire, and each breath felt like piercing knives. I needed Jesus.

In my mind's eye, I saw family members who'd passed away, and I realised they'd all died prematurely—my dad, my sister, my brother, my best friend. I shut my eyes tight. *Not me, no! I have not fulfilled my purpose yet.*

Excruciating pain seared through my body. The warm sensation of blood covered my side. Death felt so close. I was terrified, yet I knew it would be easy to escape into death.

I was suddenly presented with a simple choice but unsure where it was from. *Do you choose to live or die?*

Choosing to die felt easy, and I immediately understood that choosing to live would be hard. The worst possible scenario crossed my mind. What if I could not use my legs? What if I was paralysed? Despite the horrific thought, I felt myself say, *I choose to live.*

Louis jolted from the tractor and kneeled at my side. '*Ounooi.*' He hovered over me, his face pale. 'I'm going to turn you on your side,' he said gently.

Still trying to stop the sounds escaping my lips and with the fear of paralysis, I said, 'No, do not move me.' It was laborious to speak. Louis gently rolled me onto my right side into the recovery position, and agonising pain engulfed my body. My left arm flopped over my side. I had no control over my arm. Louis took the tie-down straps from my neck and shuffled them under my head for support. He phoned our son and asked him to ring an ambulance. Louis cupped my head in his hands, and then, he remained quiet. Very quiet. What was he not saying?

Again, that question. *Do you choose to live or die?* Dying would be easy. All I had to do was let go. *I choose to live.* I could not see my body, and I could not move. How much pain is a person able to bear and remain conscious? I thought by now I would have passed out! To take my mind off the pain and distract Louis from what was happening, I asked him in short bursts to ring our daughter and tell her not to bring the grandkids. It was their anniversary, and we'd arranged for the grandkids to stay overnight with us. Breathing became laboured, and through wheezes, I asked him to retrieve my mobile sitting on the small tractor—anything but the pain that seared through every part of me. I could barely speak. I was terrified, and this was my way of putting on a brave face. My chest was on fire, and my left side throbbed. The agony was unbearable. Time limped along. All I wanted was to pass out, but little did I know that the following hour would bring something beyond transformation. Something explosive.

The ambulance siren announced help was on its way. We were in the field, and the dirt road was some way off. They would need to carry me to the vehicle. *Maybe I should try and get up to walk to the ambulance? No, that is absurd!*

One of the paramedics introduced himself, a middle-aged man. He spoke to Louis, who said something about me being conscious.

'What is your name?' the man asked as he bent down on one knee. It was near impossible to speak as any movement forced the eerie sounds over my lips and caused incredible pain. All I wanted was for them to help me. I did not care about pleasantries.

'Maria,' I muttered.

He stood up quickly and looked at Louis. 'I have to make a phone call.'

The seconds felt like hours.

'Yes, I need urgent permission to administer morphine immediately. The patient is fully conscious and experiencing everything. Also, we will need a helicopter; she will not survive the trip in the ambulance.' I would have expected his demeanour to be neutral and poker-faced, but the urgency in his voice was unmistakable. He ended the call with one hand holding the back of his head. The paramedics spoke in inaudible, lowered voices. The man kneeled at my side again. 'Maria, we'll give you some morphine, and we will need to get a drain inserted into your side to help you breathe again, okay?'

I tried to nod. Speaking was impossible. It felt like my lungs were filling up and I was drowning. My breathing was shallow and rapid. They removed my shoes, and pain throbbed through my right leg—another injury. The paramedics turned me onto my back, and I could feel the incision in my left side, a vague burning sensation compared to the continual throbbing in my arm and chest. The uneven ground and rocks pushed into my skin, and mud and dirt clung to my legs and arms. Beads of sweat rolled down my face and neck.

My head felt dull, and my stomach nauseous. The morphine started to kick in. The paramedics cut my clothes off and moved me onto a stretcher.

I'd lost everything—my husband, my children, my career, years of things I'd done, everything I'd worked for. Even the clothes off my body—it was all gone. Death was close, and none of these things was going to be with me at the moment I died. *I needed Jesus!* I felt such a deep sense of loss but could not ponder it for long.

The helicopter landed, and my mind switched between the throbbing pain and the inevitable—I was dying. The paramedics moved me into the ambulance to get me to the helicopter in the top paddock, and I drifted in and out of consciousness. When we reached the helicopter, a doctor introduced himself. He spoke to Louis about administering anaesthetics—something about the hospital trip and chances of survival.

Everything around me became blurry, and for a third time, I was given that choice. *Do you choose to live or die?* I felt annoyed that I had to make the same choice again. *I choose to live!* At that moment, I knew everything was over. I let go. I surrendered it all. I let go of my family, my job, the good things I'd done in my life, everything I'd perceived as important.

Suddenly, my awareness changed, and I saw Jesus with me! *He was right there with me!* It was not a dream, and unlike any vision or encounter I have had before. This felt different. It felt more real than the paddock, the helicopter or anything else.

I'd always believed that the first time I saw Jesus face-to-face would look different—me in a pretty white dress, smiling; and he waiting for me, arms outstretched. Yet here I was—naked, covered in mud and blood with my body crushed in, God knows, how many places.

The most profound and life-changing moment of my life, so I would learn later, eventuated over the next few seconds—or minutes—I am unsure how long it was exactly. I was told I had to be revived in the helicopter three times, and whether I left my body, or my body left me, I could not tell. All I know is I was still me. Frankly, I did not care about time or dying or anything else, but that moment—that beautiful moment of rebirth.

12

THE CALL

Parts of the following have been voiced by my daughter, Louise, to remain faithful to the flow of events, as I was either unconscious or not present during some sections.

Louise on the Morning of the Accident

Dad called when I was on my way to drop the kids off at school. It is not a call you expect as part of the morning routine, and apart from, 'Mum got hurt badly,' there was not much to go on. Dad has never been a man of many words, but the intensity in his voice left a heaviness in the pit of my stomach. All I knew was that a tree was involved, and it was severe enough for an ambulance to be on the way.

It took every bit of energy to hold it together as I kissed my kids goodbye at school drop-off. My hands shook as I gripped the steering wheel and pointed the car's nose towards the farm. An icy hand clenched my heart, and I felt powerless as questions raced through my mind. All I knew to do was pray, but I could not think of the words, let alone utter something remotely lifesaving! I called my friend, Carlie, and through sobs, briefly relayed what I knew and asked her to get in contact with our group of friends for urgent prayer and for me not to get a speeding fine.

'I believe that through this, your mum is going to access Heaven and come back completely healed from rheumatoid arthritis and Hashimoto's,' Carlie said. I grabbed onto my friend's words and used them as a focus point. I had nothing else. The road seemed never-ending.

'Jesus, I do not know what to pray, but I need you right now.' Through the tears, a sudden knowingness settled in my heart. From that moment onwards, it was a fight between my mind and my heart. My mind concocted all kinds of horrible scenarios while my heart, without words, presented a silent calm. I knew Mum was going to be okay and that everything would be fine, yet I had no proof but the feeling in my heart.

I found Dad in the field next to Mum. He was waiting for the medics to load Mum into the helicopter. Without words, I walked over to him and wrapped my arms around him. I felt so sorry for him as the tears shook his body and all I could do was hold him. I cannot remember if I breathed, and every fibre of me wanted to deny that this was real. I wanted to look elsewhere, look away, change the scene, and start the day over.

Mum was lying next to the helicopter on a stretcher, wrapped up and with a mask fitted. It was obvious she was unconscious. I knelt on the grass next to Mum and kissed her forehead. 'I love you, Moekie.' My heart ripped on the inside, and I tried to stop the tears. I imagined what must be going through Dad's mind. I wanted to stop the hurt, for Mum, for Dad, for everyone, and I had to fight the urge to hurry the paramedics. I knew they were doing what they could to stabilise Mum as they checked and rechecked their instruments, but it felt like dawdling to me. The medical staff continued to work on Mum. We watched and waited. We asked a question here and there, but were mostly quiet.

Safe wings, please take care of her, I prayed in silence as we watched the helicopter take off at last for Brisbane. Dad and I left the farm and headed to the hospital.

Maria Arriving at Hospital

I remember the whirr of helicopter blades in the background and the clack of metal followed by a sharp tug. My body felt like lead, and as if it lagged by a few seconds, constantly trying to catch up to what had already happened. Silhouettes crowded my bed and interrupted flashes of flickering lights and pale walls. Abrupt exchanges in medical terms darted from one person to the next. I felt terrified, and loneliness crept over me. *What was happening?* My throat was dry, and my heart pounded in my head.

'Aunt, Miemie.' I heard the familiar voice of Anne, my niece. I did not realise she worked in this emergency department.

The intensity of the pain overwhelmed the fleeting moment of comfort. I yearned to go back to that moment with Jesus. I wanted to escape this nightmare. I closed my eyes and tried to let go of the fears that plagued my mind.

The noises faded, and the lights dimmed. I slipped away.

'Maria? Maria, can you hear me?' An unfamiliar female figure stood next to me. It was hard to open my eyes. I felt exhausted.

'Maria, you have been in an accident, and you are in the hospital. We're going to take care of you, okay?'

I tried to nod and felt the restriction of a neck brace. Panic crept over me as I became aware of strange things in my mouth, throat, and nose. I must have drifted away before. I tried to lift my right hand to reach my face but could barely move. The alarm in my eyes must have shown as the nurse leaned over and placed her hand on mine.

'You're okay, darling. You're on a ventilator to help you breathe. Take it easy. You won't be able to talk for a while.'

My mouth was thick and dry, and my tongue was like a stranger's. I tried to swallow, but something in my throat pushed back, and a burning sensation echoed in resistance. Although my head was muddled and foggy, I was acutely aware of the pain that throbbed in my left arm. I attempted to move the fingers on my left hand, and a surge of agony ran up my arm and into my shoulder. My arm was heavy, and my chest was on fire. Rhythmic blasts of air-like sounds, accompanied by involuntary breathing movements, pushed air into my chest. A machine breathed for me. I'd never felt this thirsty or tired. Why did they make the room so hot? Beads of sweat formed on my forehead and ran down my face. Apart from the nurse, there were several persons in the room. They discussed what I assumed were procedures. The doctors and specialists noticed I was awake and turned to face me. They introduced themselves. Their words became indistinguishable.

My eyelids became heavy, and I blinked slowly. The room was foggy and too hot. There were clouds near the ceiling. I blinked again. My heart longed for a familiar face. I just wanted to go back to where Jesus was. I closed my eyes and thought of Jesus' love. I slipped away, and a familiar softness gave way under my feet as a breeze frolicked through my hair. I was elsewhere.

Louise Arriving at Hospital

It felt bittersweet walking into Amarinda's embrace in the Intensive Care Unit's (ICU) waiting room. My cousin was more like a sister to Mum, and their connection was like no other. Anne was there too. Waiting. We were all waiting. A waiting room is such a cruel space. You have to keep it together there in a public room. Nod and smile, even though you are screaming inside. My jaws were aching. The gnashing was not intentional. I could not help it. My only desire was to see Mum and be by her side, to let her know we were there for her, that everything would be okay, that she was not alone. I glared at the glass doors that separated us from her. She was just there, in the next room. Why could we not go in?

My thoughts were interrupted by two men who introduced themselves as doctors. Dad and I jumped up. A short handshake and a nod later, Dad, Amarinda, Anne, and I were invited into a small conference room. I felt relieved to finally hear from someone, but anxious at the same time. I looked at the doctors. They seemed so young, or were they? How much experience did they have? It was my mum we were talking about here. Her life. *Our* lives. It was comforting to have Anne there, even if it was just to translate the medical jargon and answer our questions. What a Godsend that she worked at this hospital at this time! It was another ray of hope I could grab and stuff in my pocket for later.

'The team of doctors looking after your mum is some of the best in the country. She is in good hands.' Anne whispered as if she read my mind. I forced a brief smile and sat down.

'Maria sustained multiple serious injuries through the blunt trauma to her chest and left side, but we are happy that she is currently stable,' the doctor said. 'She has been placed in an induced coma and is under constant observation here in ICU. In a situation like Maria's, we assess all the injuries sustained and then address the most urgent issues first to ensure the best-case scenario. Her breathing was the priority. She is currently on a ventilator, which means we are helping her with her breathing as she has a punctured lung.' We listened quietly.

The doctor touched his right shoulder and spoke in a calm voice. 'The humeral head, or ball of the shoulder, which provides movement to the arm, was shattered by the impact and moved into the space where her armpit is. We are concerned that it could permanently damage the nerves, which will prevent her from using her arm if we do not act soon. We would like to operate tonight to reconstruct the humorous head and get it back into position.' We all nodded and listened in silence. I held my breath. From the little I knew of the medical field, I knew that anything like internal bleeding or organ damage was something we did not want as part of the conversation. Apart from the punctured lung already mentioned, I quietly prayed that all other injuries would be less serious.

The doctor continued. 'Her upper left arm has a clean fracture, and her shoulder has been dislocated. Other injuries include multiple rib fractures from the impact on her chest and side. All but the top and bottom ribs on her left have multiple fractures, with some ribs up to five fractures. On her right side, there are a couple of fractures too. This complicates breathing as there is no support to help lift her rib cage. The T8 on her spine is fractured, but we have not got a full assessment on this yet, so at this stage, it is being treated with caution, and Maria will be log rolled.' He looked at each of us as he spoke, so well composed. It took a few moments to get my head around it all, and I sighed as he continued.

'Also, Maria's right knee cap has been fractured and needs reconstruction. Her pelvis has a small fracture. It is probably one of the most severe cases we have seen, but given Maria's health, she has a good chance of recovery. As I have mentioned, our priority would be the shoulder, and then we will see how stable she is after the operation before moving to the next issue.'

Dad signed some paperwork to okay the procedures, and we were allowed to go into ICU to see Mum. My legs shook, and my heart sank when I laid eyes on her. I could barely recognise her amongst all the wires and pipes. Her skin was an eerie pale grey, and she was damp with sweat. It felt strange to touch her hand like it was not my mum lying there, even though the beeping monitors indicated otherwise. For a while, I did not want to look at her, was unsure where to turn my head, like it was wrong to look. The room reeked of ether or some cleaning chemical.

'She can hear you,' said the nurse at her bedside.

I gently kissed Mum on her forehead. 'I love you, Moekie.' Sweat clung to my lips, but her eyes remained closed, and there was no response to my whisper. Dad's eyes filled with tears as he gently stroked her hair. Dad and I avoided eye contact as our emotions welled up. We only had a few minutes as the staff needed to prepare her for surgery. It was time to go.

Maria Prior to Shoulder Surgery

'Maria.' I vaguely heard the nurse say my name. It was a challenge to focus. 'Maria, your family is here to see you.' I tried to open my eyes.

'Hi, Moekie.' I heard my daughter's voice and looked to my right. Her fingers wrapped around my hand. My arms wanted to hug her, and my mouth wanted to say the words, *It would be all right.* But, instead, my eyelids were heavy, and my mouth paralysed. Louis stood on my left, and I could feel his pain as he stroked my hair. I felt so sorry for them. What were they going through seeing me like this?

Louis leaned over. 'They're going to start the shoulder surgery soon, so we can't stay.' I heard the words, but the meaning felt strange. The objects in my mouth restricted the smile I attempted.

'Maria, we are going to check your vitals. Nod if you can hear me.' My head dipped once as I looked at the doctor. It hurt so much. My mouth felt ill-fitting. Dry. Everything hurt. *What are they doing with my arm? When did my family disappear?* I felt annoyed as more and more of me ached.

The room was darker than before. *It must be night. If only my family were here now.* I felt so alone, and the heat was intolerable. How I longed for my family to put a cold washer on me, to just be there beside me. My body felt heavy and my head thick.

'Maria, the specialists are ready for you. We are moving you into surgery now.'

The bed's wheels became an instrument of relentless torture as each little bump and adjustment echoed in piercing pain and reminded me of every broken part. The pain throbbed from my arm, swelled into my chest, and engulfed my body until I was in an ocean of anguish.

It became too much to endure, and I gave up my last breath. I felt to drown would save me from this torment. I involuntarily gasped for more air. Instead of oxygen, the blackness around me filled my lungs and stung like a million needles which spread quickly to each part of my body. Another wave of pain consumed me as the process started again.

Finally, they stopped moving the bed!

'Maria, we are giving you some pain meds as well as anaesthetic now.'

A frown replaced the temporary relief as I looked around me. *How would a surgeon be able to work in this dark room? Why are there no lights?* The place reminded me of an underground cellar with no windows, and the dark cement walls and stained roof eerily stared back at me in silence. A strong smell of ether made my head throb with dizziness. Panic crept up in me, and I swallowed hard. The pipe in my throat pushed back, reminding me that I could not scream. I tried to lift my hands to pull the tube out, but my arms felt like lead, and my body remained motionless no matter how hard I tried to move. Beads of sweat ran down the sides of my face and pooled behind my neck.

Oh, someone! Please! Why am I here? I squinted to distinguish the shapes in the room and heard a groaning noise. *Is it from a nearby bed?* I could not make out what I heard. I tried to hold my breath to listen, but the ventilator forced air into my lungs.

It felt as if my heart would pound through my chest. Why was I alone? Where is everyone? Waves of heat washed up more panic as a horrible thought crossed my mind. *Can it be? No! What if...?*

I tried to shuffle position to eliminate the thought in my head, but my body did not respond. Darkness crept closer and stole the last bit of air from the room. I tried to turn my head, but in vain. My body was melted into position, and I was compelled to deal with the terror that forced itself into my reality.

I have been moved to an underground storage area for ICU patients—to die. Just left here to die...

It all made perfect sense. ICU patients are a considerable expense for the hospital, and if they could get us to die sooner... This room...

The anguish and horror overwhelmed me and pushed down on my chest like an invisible force that drained the life from me.

If only I could die! Anything would be better than this! My eyes would not close, my limbs laid heavy, and the darkness became thick like smoke. The burden of my body's weight and the force on my chest intensified. The room faded.

Louise

Anne and her hubby offered their place for us to stay on Friday night. We were exhausted. There was nothing more we could do but keep our hopes up. I reread and reread all the messages of encouragement and prayer from our group of friends. Never have I needed them so much, appreciated each word so much. I curled up into bed and allowed the tears to flow where no one could watch. In my mind's eye, I could see Mum, and all I wanted to do was hug her, tell her we were close. I expanded my spirit out like I could reach her, I tried to comfort her, and instead, I was met by a huge bear hug from her. At first, I was shocked and then relaxed into her hug and almost immediately fell asleep. Mum was okay; at least her spirit was okay.

I woke up at 2 am on Saturday and rang the hospital to check how Mum was doing. She was stable, and the nurse said she'd slept for most of the night. She mentioned that Mum would be a bit drowsy after the operation, and we should keep that in mind when we came in to see her later that morning. Anne had told us the night before that the doctors did their rounds early morning, and there was not much point in going to the hospital before 7 am as they would not allow us to see Mum before then. The clock ticked along slowly, and it left Dad and me with time to try and process things. He sat on the couch, staring at nothing in particular, and every few minutes, shook his head, let out a deep sigh and shuffled in his seat. I placed a cup of tea in front of him on the coffee table.

'Dad, what are you thinking?' His eyes focused as he reached for the tea, and another deep sigh filled the air.

'I am trying to find an answer. Why? Why would this happen?' I could feel his words echo inside me. I sat down on the couch opposite him and took a sip of tea. I, too, had been mulling over the events, trying to make sense of it all.

'There must be some sort of meaning to all this. How else would we survive it? Or anyone survive something like this?' I said. I wanted to be a support for my dad, as I could feel the heaviness of the pain he carried. I could not even start to imagine what he must be going through. He has seen the accident from start to finish, and there was nothing he could do to stop it.

'If only I could have a rewind button, just reverse that one moment,' Dad said. That moment of the accident replayed in his mind and tormented his emotions.

'All I know is that this was not something God did,' I replied. 'It could not be. The only thing that makes sense to me is that Mum would have chosen this a long time ago before we were even on Earth. And I chose to be her daughter, and you chose to be her husband. We must have chosen this because we knew the good that would come from this. We must have been sitting with Jesus and seen the result. There must be something amazing that will come from all this. Otherwise, it is not worth it.' I reasoned out loud. I did not know how to focus on anything, how to hear Jesus in amongst all of this, or how to pray. I did not have any answers for Dad or myself. I felt so small and alone. All I wanted was to clutch at anything that would bring some sort of hope.

At that moment, my phone beeped. I tried to read the messages from our group of friends aloud to Dad to encourage him, but my voice was shaky. Many people were praying for us, and as I read the words, my awareness suddenly shifted. Instead of feeling like it was Dad and I fighting against the circumstances, I could sense our friends, family, and then I could feel Jesus, Papa, Holy Spirit, and the angels. Suddenly I just knew all of Heaven was there on this journey with us. No matter how the circumstances looked, we were not alone. I breathed in hope and courage.

'Dad, one of my friends suggested we take the memory of the accident and give it to Jesus. Then Jesus can make something from it. Would you be okay to do this?'

'Yes.' He nodded.

In faith, we stood up and said a simple prayer. We stepped into Jesus, and Dad gave the accident, along with all the emotions and trauma, to Jesus. Tears rolled down his cheeks, and I could feel the heaviness lift from the room. There was hope. Not in the circumstances, but higher up, bigger than us. We could hold on to something no matter what we heard or saw. We were ready.

Dad later told me that he saw green pastures, and from that moment onwards, he could talk about the accident without reliving it the way he did before.

13

RAIN AND BANANAS

Louise

Dad and I stayed by Mum's side every second we were allowed to be there. ICU became a familiar place, and over the next few days, we held our breath and tears more times than we could count. Other times the emotion would just swamp us, and tears would flow spontaneously.

Neither of us ever spoke this out loud, I think we did not dare to, but we both thought the 'what if' questions. What if Mum could not walk again? What if she needed permanent care? What if…? It was less a concerning 'what if' for us because I am sure we would have worked out any number of ways to take care of her. The 'what if' was with her in mind.

Mum has always been independent and, dare I say, a bit proud. Not that she ever thought she was better than another living soul. No, it was more that she would be pressed to ask for help. It was the kind of pride that would let her suffer in silence to avoid the likelihood of being a burden on someone else. It is a selfless kind of pride, if such a thing exists. I knew she was a fighter, and the very fact that she was still alive was proof enough. What grated at my insides was what I could not see. What was going on inside her mind? What was she thinking about when she was conscious?

My heart sank as I recalled how she'd responded to similar situations in the past. Nothing I remembered brought me closer to peace. Mum once broke her shoulder when we were in a car accident. I do not know if she meant it, but she said she wished she'd died in that car accident. There was an awkward silence after she said it. I do not think Dad knew how to respond. Everything just got a bit much for her that day. We'd rolled the car on our return from holidays a few weeks earlier, and a piece of bone chipped off her shoulder, leaving her right arm incapacitated. It was not the pain she could not handle—it was the inability to get little things done that frustrated her most. Everything a right-handed person would need their right arm for, such as getting dressed and preparing dinner. She struggled through it without asking for help unless she had no choice. I believe she despised asking for help. At the time, all three of us kids were in primary school, and Mum owned an accounting business. She had a lot to take care of without the inconvenience of a broken shoulder.

Now here she was in ICU, and machines breathed for her. For us, the hope was that she would be okay, that she would survive. For her? I think I knew what she would rather want, but my mind could not conceive of the idea. It broke my heart just wondering what was going on inside her mind.

Dad and I tried to be brave. Shaky smiles, and lots of cold washers on her forehead and left arm—now swollen three times its size—became the norm. When Mum was conscious, we would ask questions and get her to blink once for 'yes' and twice for 'no' to determine her pain level and work out what she needed. It exhausted both her and us, and when we finally worked out what she'd tried to indicate, I would break down in tears—in relief that we could help her and in frustration that something as small as an adjustment on her arm brace took so many guesses. Every time I looked into her eyes, I wondered what was going on behind them, but a big part of me did not really want to know. What if it was not what I wanted to hear? All I wanted was for her to get better, but what if she did not want to be here?

With all the braces and tubes, and all the injured parts, it was hard to know where to focus. One time, Dad and I both tried to hold her legs down as she seemed to be dreaming and made a big jumping motion. We looked at each other wide-eyed. Her knee was shattered and her foot injured, yet here she was, obviously not present, a smile on her face and legs moving. What was she up to?

Dad and I grabbed hold of each glimmer of hope we could find and upheld it like a beacon. We sent messages to friends and family with updates on Mum's progress. We reread and reread the replies of prayers and encouragement. I decided to buy a journal from a shop inside the hospital and capture the messages we received and sent. Many of them were for Mum, and she could not read them. Not yet. If I wrote them down and it was something for her to read later, she had to wake up to do so, right?

Mum was in a coma most of the time. I moved to the head of her bed, behind the machines that kept her alive, to not disrupt the nurses and doctors. Uninterrupted blocks of time seemed non-existent with the constant monitoring. I needed her to hear the messages so she would know that a large group of people believed and prayed, that she was not alone, and that she would have support when she woke. I was not sure if she could hear anything, but if she did, maybe it would bring her hope as it had for us. I needed her to not give up.

I bent down and spoke into her ear.

'Mum, I'm going to read you some of the messages from everyone praying for you.' It was hard as I choked up most of the time, but I kept going because it meant I could talk to her, and it was not hospital-related; it was about hope.

The messages consisted of healing prayers for Mum and thoughts for us. Some were spot-on. The day after the accident, I read the following to Mum:

'Carlie sent a message saying that she feels healing is going to happen quicker than expected. That you will see that Jesus has always, always been completely in love with you. This is going to be beautiful in so many ways. She is praying that you are enjoying every moment with Jesus right now and that you will remember it. She also wrote that she is praying for healing for you, but instead of just healing the injuries, that you would be completely and totally healed from all the sickness and come back completely new and whole.'

Mum showed no response as I read, but I refused to give up.

'Callie said that you came into her head quite vividly when she prayed, and she was shocked when she heard what happened until the Lord reminded her of how you were the day we prayed for you at Carlie's (about a month before). You had the weight of the world on your shoulders. You had done the courts of heaven, done the DNA, and she felt the Lord said 'ENOUGH!' You were burdened with doing everything to make things better. Callie wrote that while she had you in her heart yesterday and last night, she felt strongly that HE is making all things new in you—you are weak and vulnerable at the moment, and his strength and power will manifest through your vulnerability. How he loves you!!'

Each time the doctors scheduled a procedure, we asked for prayer, and as each one was labelled a success by the team of doctors, we celebrated each small step and allowed ourselves to breathe a little. Moments away from Mum felt like slow motion, yet in these moments, we felt Jesus, and the warmth of the support and love spilled over from all the prayers.

Some might argue that we tried to find Jesus in a very desperate situation, but I believe it truly was all of Heaven making itself known to us. The little things felt huge and left a deep imprint of how involved Heaven was in our lives—little things like rain and breakfast.

Although the hospital was over two hours from home, the generosity of friends had us travel only 20 minutes each day to be with Mum. We parked some distance from the hospital and then walked the rest of the way to save on the hospital's extravagant parking costs. After a few days of sunshine, we greeted a rainy morning, and as we looked for a park, we realised that we had a ten-minute walk ahead of us without umbrellas. I uttered a simple one-liner prayer out loud, 'Please let the rain stop for just ten minutes!'

It could not be a coincidence that we stepped through the automatic doors of the hospital entrance completely dry, and then looked at each other in surprise when it started raining again seconds later.

Breakfast was the same yogurt and muesli we had been having for the last few days, and I mentioned to Dad how good a banana would be to mix things up. I walked over to the vending machines. A lady was busy restocking the fruit section, so I asked if I could purchase some bananas as the vending machine was not in use. She handed me a packet of bananas, said that they were set aside as they were slightly damaged. It was free, and the bananas were perfect.

At that stage, I quickly exchanged coincidence for supernatural intervention and felt that the little things in our lives mattered to Jesus, that he was trying to tell us everything would be okay. We were not just looked after—we were being taken care of, which made us feel loved.

A few days after the accident, Carlie and her sister visited us in the ICU waiting area. They came to support Dad and me—a welcome change of routine.

'It was strange when you asked me to pray for your mum,' Carlie said.

'Strange?'

'Yeah, I knew that the situation was serious, and I got ready to pray this serious prayer for healing, but I could not.'

'Did you not know what to pray?'

'I saw your mum in Heaven, and she was having so much fun. I have never seen her with so much joy. I was almost jealous! She was surrounded in the brightest light, much brighter than I had ever seen before. We were so happy to see each other, and she looked amazing—free and joyful without any worries.'

I smiled as I listened to Carlie and then cried. 'She is okay?'

'She is having the best time with Jesus! And when I saw her, I could not pray this serious prayer. I ended up praying something simple like a child's prayer and instead thanked Jesus for all the joy she would bring back with her.'

When Carlie shared what she saw, I wanted it to be true with all my heart. I wanted my mind to believe it. Was Mum aware of any of this? Was she in Heaven because her body was dying? Would she come back to us?

14

WE HAVE NO IDEA

Louise

The day the doctors announced that Mum showed signs of independent breathing and the ventilator would be removed, I felt absolutely terrified and ecstatic at the same time. She was getting better; that was clear and wonderful. Every day we celebrated the small things. The arm operation was a success, then wiring the rib case back together, and then the knee. Today we were told that they would remove her breathing pipe so she could now breathe for herself. My heart did a mini celebration, and I felt so grateful—one step closer to recovery.

What I was unsure of was the approaching moment of truth. Up to now, we only guessed what Mum could be thinking. Her blinks to respond 'yes' or 'no' were in response to physical help. The most terrifying idea would be that Mum had morbid thoughts. What if she could not stand this? What if she hated the dependency so much that she did not want to live? We could fix a dressing or give painkillers, but we could not fix how she thought or responded. With that in the forefront of my mind, I walked into the hospital, well aware that, for the first time, Mum would be able to do more than blink.

The doors opened, and allowing us access into the ICU, but my legs needed help to walk. I desperately wanted to see Mum, but I did not. Dad and I were silent as we walked down the corridor. Nothing we could have said to each other would have changed what we would experience next. We turned the corner at the end of the aisle and headed towards Mum. A nurse stood next to her bed and another near the foot of the bed. The curtains were half-drawn, so I could not see Mum immediately. I could feel my heartbeat and wondered if everyone else could hear how loud it was. I swung my handbag from my shoulder and aimed to make my way around the nurse towards Mum.

I searched for Mum's face. When I met her gaze, it was like a ton of concrete dropped off my heart. She was semi-upright in bed, and gone were the pipes that covered her nose and mouth. Her eyes were filled with tears as she met us with a tender smile. The pale grey skin gave way to a slight yellow tinge, with a bit of colour on her cheeks. She looked so much better, but I knew it was not the lack of grey or the tinge of yellow on her skin, nor was it the missing tubes. I could not distinguish what it was at that moment, as I had no time to ponder the thought.

I rushed to her side, 'Oh, Moekie.' Tears streamed freely as I held her hand and stated the obvious. 'The pipes are gone! Yay!'

She looked at me, and in a soft, gravelly voice, said the words that brought utter relief to my soul.

I knew she was talking about Jesus, and more than that, I knew she was okay. Her emotional and mental state was okay. Her eyes smiled even though I could tell she was exhausted. Mum said nothing else during that visit, but we did not need to hear anything else. If I could label a day, I would write the letters G- R-E-A-T in the sky for this day.

Maria

It was a process to get used to the frailness of my strength and what my body could endure. The pain and interrupted rest, as procedures and nurse duties took preference over anything else, were exhausting. The ventilator had finally come off, five days after the accident, and although I was delighted at the removal of the obstructions from my airway, breathing on my own was more taxing than I had imagined. I quickly realised that a short sentence was about all I could manage before I needed rest. A yearning burned inside me to share what I had experienced since the moment I had passed out next to the helicopter. That one moment had changed everything for me, and the events that followed were frustrated by my body's limitations. I could not wait for the early morning check-ups to be over so that my family could walk in, and I could finally share some of it with them. I stared at the clock on the wall and sighed. The movement hurt my chest, and I closed my eyes for a moment.

I felt entangled by the to and fro of my inner dialogue, like a tug of rope contest balancing what my body could physically cope with and what I wanted to share. Then there was the analysis of what I could share and what I should share, or more importantly, what I should not share. I must have gone over the scenarios and considered each possibility a thousand times. I did not want to come across as crazy or delusional.

Someone told me that the painkillers could cause hallucinations. I had the strongest sense that what I'd experienced were not hallucinations, except for the single experience of being left in an underground storage area. That one experience felt different from everything else I had felt and seen and been immersed in over the last few days.

When the world became a blur in the field where the accident happened, I knew full well that the cause was morphine. As I slipped in and out of consciousness, I questioned what was real and what was not more times than I cared to mention, as everything did not just go black. My saving grace, the moment that has engulfed all of what I understood to be real, the moment that has left me thinking and yearning for nothing else, the moment I believe has saved my life, the one thing I kept going back to—this was the moment I experienced when the world faded. This was what I needed to share with my family. With anyone who would care to listen. Could I trust myself to make sense? To be coherent? An overwhelming number of experiences boiled down to the one sentence I could muster when my family finally walked into the ICU that morning. 'We have no idea how much he loves us.'

I did not know where to start, what to share, what to say, what not to say. The only thing that came to mind was the one thing that burned inside me, the one thing that kept drawing me back, that changed everything I knew or thought I knew.

A few days previously, on the day I had died, I had briefly woken up after the helicopter landed at the hospital. I was aware of being moved into the hospital, and the awareness of my body became too heavy. When I woke up, the pain was so immense; all I wanted was to be back with Jesus. That single thought and that single desire immediately drew me back somehow, and I slipped away as the hospital room faded fast. I could not explain what was happening at the time, but knew that I was no longer aware of any pain or the hospital or the medical staff trying to save my life.

The sensation I experienced was similar to being drawn into something, not unlike falling, but more intentional. My stomach felt a familiar tightening while my skin tingled, and the rush of adrenaline manifested through my senses long before my mind worked out I was on a slide. The slide's speed and excitement gave me such a thrill, and I enjoyed the moment, being fully present. With my arms in the air and my legs outstretched, I followed the slide around and downwards, and the narrower the spiral became, the faster I went down the slide and the more the excitement built. At the core of the slide, with great speed accompanied by a jubilant wheeeeee! and a big jump, I landed in a chair at a massive white table. Utterly delighted and surprised at the thrill and the sight in front of me, I looked around to see familiar faces around the table, all joyous and in a celebratory mood. People were clinking glasses and delighting in the meticulously adorned table, which could only be described as a feast. The contrast from immense pain and thirst to this celebration confounded me; however, it did not hold me back, and I indulged in the warm bread and juiciest fruit. What astounded me was that the food that entered my body had an immediate healing effect. I cried with happiness.

And then nothing more mattered as the mere sight of Jesus at the table, celebrating with us, was enough to overwhelm my heart, and my insides collapsed into an emotional mess of gratefulness, excitement, and a strength I had not known before this moment. The joy around us was tangible and contagious. How could one heart hold so many different emotions at the same time? The atmosphere was unlike anything I could have imagined. Here—wherever this was—I had the sense that each individual was esteemed, noticed, worthy, yet no single individual was more important than another. It was not about one person.

I popped another grape into my mouth and felt the refreshing sweetness soothe my dry throat while every part of me soaked up the welcoming warmth, laughter, and happy chatter that filled the atmosphere.

'Maria.'

I could feel the tug, but everything in me wanted to fight it.

'Maria, can you hear me?'

No. Do not take me away from this!

Pain.

No!

I found myself back in the hospital room. The throbbing in my arm and burning in my chest made my heart beat faster, and through blinks, I noticed a figure next to my bed. Lights flickered. *Why is it so hot in here?*

A nurse spoke and said something about my family. It was then that I woke and realised for the first time that I was hooked up to a ventilator, and the staff started to prepare me for my first emergency surgery on my arm. The anaesthetic did not make my world go black as I had imagined it would. It did not provide me with a peaceful nothing-ness as a means of a break from the pain. It did not do what I had imagined at all. Instead of fading into welcome oblivion, the world around me suddenly became crisp and bright, with colours and lights twirling and floating around me. I had the strongest sense that I was somewhere familiar. Somewhere heaven-like.

CLOUDS AND GARDENS

I was aware of the emotions and serenity of the atmosphere long before the rest of my senses ascertained what had occurred. Jesus was with me again, and my heart jumped in surprise. His presence was so tangible, and it dawned on me that I had my head against his chest. It was like my senses woke up little by little, and elation flooded my being. I kept my eyes shut and wished for the moment to linger so that I would never forget it. There could be no better place than this, right here in Jesus' presence! I slowly opened my eyes and lifted my chin to look up at him. I was extra careful not to disturb this precious moment. As my eyes met his, Jesus smiled at me. I almost felt surprised that Jesus was still there! A mixture of disbelief and delight raced through my being. He felt tangible, and nothing about this seemed to resemble a dream. It was all too real. It was different.

Everything I experienced was multiplied by a thousand compared to what I would see and feel on Earth. It was as if a refreshing breeze filled my heart with peace and delight. I still struggle to find the words to accurately describe Jesus' presence and my sense of where I was or what was happening. Jesus was all-consuming. His presence washed through me like waves spilling into me. I could feel each cell in my being respond to his light and life. Colours streamed from him and into me, and the light was in him and around him and in me and around me. I was part of the colours and light, and they were part of me. I could not distinguish one specific colour; they moved and changed all the time.

We were in a garden, one like nothing I had seen before. I unashamedly gawked as I looked around, still clinging to Jesus. The magnificence of the space and the spectacular colours left me dumbfounded. There was so much to absorb—the radiant green of the grass, the extrinsic colours of the trees and flowers, the mountains in the distance—all more alive than anything I have known before. I stared in complete wonder at what seemed like a scene from a movie, filtered and edited to perfection. The magnificence of what was before me confounded me, as I could see every single thing in minute detail while all of the garden was near and far away at the same time. I could see the details of the mountain in the distance as if it was close to my face. Space or reach did not seem to be the same concept here as on Earth; I sensed I could access the flowers near my feet at the same time as the mountain in the distance.

Everything in the garden had a light of its own as if the light originated inside it instead of reflecting off its surface. In a garden bed nearby grew flowers the colour of a copper-peach sunset, but unlike anything I have seen on Earth. The colours were like a million colours that blended and moved, so vivid that they seemed more real than anything I have known. Petals adorned the flowers' prominent faces, and I perceived them as smiling. I slowly let go of Jesus' hand and moved closer to have a look. The flowers leaned over to touch my skin as if they welcomed me. I looked around in astonishment and then at Jesus. This garden was indeed alive, not just living! I was surrounded by a garden that breathed and responded with a life of its own. I basked in the beauty and peacefulness of the moment.

Jesus moved with me, and he seemed to enjoy my curiosity and obvious surprise. We walked from garden bed to garden bed and across a gorgeous arched bridge to the opposite side of the river. The mountains in the distance somehow drew my attention, and as I watched, a large, beautiful being approached. My first reaction was to grab Jesus' arm with both my hands, flabbergasted at the sight of this strange but stunning being. Jesus laughed, and I realised there was no danger. I relaxed a little. By now, the being was close to us and had lowered his whole body, slowly approaching. He tried to make himself seem smaller so as not to startle me. Jesus, still chuckling, reached out and ran his hand across his neck and back and gave him a familiar pat. I carefully stepped forward and reached one hand out towards the being, and looked into his eyes. To my surprise, all I could sense was love. The softness that met my fingertips as I brushed over his head and neck matched his gentle eyes, and I knew this was my friend. In this garden, we did not seem to need words, I just knew, and Jesus also knew. It was the same with this exquisite being. We spoke heart to heart. I sensed that I could climb on his back and ride with him. Without hesitation, I climbed up and wrapped my arms around his soft neck. He lifted up and up, and we flew towards the mountains. I felt a familiar glee and enjoyed the freedom.

When I woke up after surgery, it felt quite the opposite of waking from sleep. It was like I woke up into a nightmare as I became aware of my body again. I loathed it. Moments before, I was completely weightless, and it felt like I could float and fly at will. My concerns and worries, the intense pain, the negative thoughts, all of these things were non-existent in the spiritual world. While I was with Jesus, I was immersed in love and love only. I enjoyed the light that consumed me, the colours that mesmerised me, the soothing breeze, and the garden's healing tranquillity. Life emanated from every particle that surrounded me.

And then I was compelled to exchange the weightlessness for the burden of my broken body, which went hand in hand with excruciating pain, intense heat, and sweating. I was weighed down into one position, and it felt like I was fitted with a heavy straitjacket.

I realised Louis and Louise were there, and all I wanted to do was tell them that I would be okay, that I was with my Lord Jesus. I wanted to tell them about the garden and the single most significant experience I'd had with Jesus, but could not speak. I could not move. I could feel a tear run down my face, and all I could do was hope that my eyes would somehow let them know everything was going to be fine. The effort it took to stay awake and the weight of the emotions in the room utterly exhausted me, and I felt that familiar tug that drew me in. Without reservation, I surrendered to it.

I was barefoot. I know because my feet touched the familiar grass and its softness and life seemed to flow from each blade into my being. I was in that beautiful garden again. I was there in all of who I am. My entire being was still me, yet I had none of my body's pain or limitations. I felt weightless and fearless. I knew whoever I was in this place was the real me, the being that Jesus created me to be. I was fascinated by this state of being, ready to take on anything! I felt such fullness of joy, lighter than I have ever been.

There was no breeze, yet it was refreshing just to stand on the grass and take in the landscape. I breathed in deeply, held my breath for a couple of seconds, breathed out and smiled. There was no pain in my chest. Each new breath I drew felt like it absorbed some sort of tangible glimmer—it filtered into every part of me. It was invigorating, and I could not contain myself. I lifted my arms and twirled on the grass. As the garden swirled past, I caught a glimpse of two angels, their smiles beamed as they watched me slow to a standstill. Slightly startled, I stared in admiration. One angel looked familiar, and his smile could not hide the sparkle in his eyes. The other angel, a bit taller than the first, had a sense of stature and kindness. I understood that these angels were my angels. Before I could strike up a conversation, the little arched bridge in the background suddenly felt much closer, and I focused on it. Excitement bubbled up in me. Jesus was walking towards us across the bridge!

I turned and ran towards him, arms open, not a care in the world. I simultaneously laughed and cried as I met his hug and felt his arms fold over me. We walked across the bridge together, and I was aware of the angels close by my side. We did not talk. It did not seem strange not to. We knew each other's thoughts and feelings as if they were outside of our beings. We just soaked up the beauty of the garden, and new joy and life flowed through me.

The times I woke up in my body in the hospital bed became less of a shock, as I knew what to expect. Each time I returned from the garden, I brought something of the presence and atmosphere with me, and I could feel my physical body respond. I made quick progress, and surgery after surgery was successful. I needed less and less medication for the pain. What I could not settle my mind on at the time was whether the garden and Jesus were hallucinations, a by-product of the strong medication. I wanted to be taken off the strong medication as soon as possible and decided to deal with the pain by going to this spiritual world instead.

As much as I would love to live in what I experienced as Heaven, I did not want it to continue if it was caused by any drugs and was not real. What was the point in seeing and hearing things if it was not going to last, no matter how amazing? When the nurses asked what my pain level was, I minimised it. It worked, and they lowered the medication.

I was careful to analyse each experience. When the experiences did not change as the medication was lowered, I felt such relief and excitement. It energised me.

Even after I re-examined each experience, the only one that seemed odd was the single time I thought I was left in an underground storage area. That felt dark and sinister, while every other experience involved Jesus, an amazing spiritual world and the gardens, which felt light and alive, more real than the hospital or anything else. I did not understand much of it, but I could feel the life I brought back into my body each time I returned from these Heavenly encounters. 'Waking up' usually refers to reality, but reality felt numb, flat, and colourless.

When I was conscious, my mind would analyse the experiences.

What would be considered sane to share and what would be thought of as crazy? Deep inside, I wondered if my family would think I had gone mad and that the best place after the hospital would be a mental institution. I knew that I was not crazy, but would they think otherwise? I desperately needed some confirmation that I was not the only person who'd experienced what felt more real and true than anything this world contained. At this time, I was still on the ventilator, so speaking or asking questions was not an option. As I pondered these things, I slipped away into the garden again.

The familiar yearning to be with Jesus drew me back, and I could not wait to feel the life this spiritual world offered. On this particular day, I was consumed by the magnificence of the garden and the water flowing through it. The pebbles on the river bed were as visible and bright as if I was holding some of them in my hand. I watched from the side of the river and tried to study the variety of colours as I soaked up the life that emanated from it, when I felt that tug again—an involuntary movement as if I was drawn backwards into a cloud. It was strange to feel it here in this spiritual dimension, as I was used to the reverse—when I was in my body in the hospital bed, I got accustomed to being drawn into another dimension, yet here I felt the tug again. It felt like I was in two places at once. A part of me was lost in total admiration and awe and floated in a space where time did not matter, and gravity had no effect, where everything seemed surreal and light, like in a dream, but more authentic than anything I had known before. Another part of me heeded the gentle tug that caused the involuntary movement. I was torn between two worlds, and I could feel my spirit in the process of floating back into my body while I still stared at the magnificent surroundings.

'Miemie?'

I heard my name and opened my eyes, but somehow two worlds overlapped and intertwined, and for the next few minutes, my brain struggled to make sense of what was going on. I was still moving and not quite awake, as I could feel my spirit had not settled into my body yet. It was a weird sensation, moving while lying still, trying to catch up with yourself. It was at this moment that I opened my eyes. I expected to see the hospital room, but instead, I was in the most astonishing garden filled with flowers and arrangements like I had never seen before. This was not the same place I had come from just moments before. The colours were unique, and the flowers incomparable to what I have ever known. The beauty of this garden was so different from my garden, and yet felt familiar somehow. It was evident that this talented gardener had designed every detail and spent many hours here to maintain its magnificence. The uniqueness of the flowers and the way they were arranged felt like a story, a life. I looked around and could see parts of the garden were well-established, with large trees and impressive flower beds, while others were new with smaller plants. Other sections were still piles of dirt where garden beds were in progress. I was trying to work out how I had never seen these flowers and arrangements before, yet it all seemed strangely intimate and familiar.

In the hospital room, my niece, Amarinda, was bending over my bed and gently calling my name while looking at me. Some part of me did not see her face or eyes or anything in the hospital room.

'Oh gosh, she is looking into my soul!' Amarinda placed her hand over her tummy, and her eyes widened.

I recognised Amarinda's voice and focused. My heart leapt as mixed emotions danced inside of me. A deep desire to ask forgiveness for what had just happened intertwined with the exuberant joy that someone outside of me had just confirmed that my experiences were real. For the first time since the accident, there was some evidence that I was not delusional or crazy! All of the gardens and angels and experiences with Jesus were real!

My brain slowly tried to process what had just happened. *Oh, wow! I did not realise we could see into each other's gardens!* Then the details in the garden made sense. Of course! The beauty of Amarinda, the arrangements, her life, her story, I knew each part of it so well but had never imagined it could be so beautifully displayed.

Words were not an option, thanks to the tube in my throat, so I looked at Amarinda and tried to say *I am so sorry* with my eyes, unsure if I had trespassed into her garden, yet overwhelmed by the beauty of it all.

Between the tears, and while I thanked Jesus for this awe-inspiring moment, I was back with my angels again, as I simply learned to let go when I felt the tug.

I do not know how I ended up in this place. All I did was let go. I felt the tug and gave in to it. I drew my breath with such force, it was audible, and my jaw dropped. I stared. The more I saw, the more I gawked.

I was not in my garden; that was for sure!

Multiple gardens surrounded me, as far as I could see. These gardens were in mid-air and grew and shaped while I looked at them. They moved upwards and spiralled towards the sky, sideways and downwards. As I moved between the floating gardens, I noticed they were all Fibonacci spirals—perfectly balanced according to the divine proportion, similar to the arrangements of a pinecone or the flowering of an artichoke or the spiral on some snail shells, except they were hundreds of times larger!

Each garden had arrangements of incredible trees, shrubs, flowers, and plants that composed a perfect balance. It was evident that someone had precisely positioned each living thing—it was by design. Nothing here seemed random. Flowers blossomed into incredible colours, trees expanded, and various plants filled the spaces to reveal intricate patterns on the larger spirals. The phenomenon of the display overwhelmed my senses.

I found it mind-boggling. If compared, the most incredible botanical garden on Earth would seem flat, as these gardens grew in multiple dimensions, upwards, outwards, sideways, intertwined and interconnected. Each plant had a specific purpose, formed part of an incredible tapestry. I discovered new dimensions the more I moved about, adding to my fascination, and I gaped shamelessly.

Maybe I was somewhere on Earth? The gardens felt familiar, like known places, but that was impossible. It felt plausible that each garden could resemble a project of sorts, and the thought filled me with excitement. The beauty and incredible potential represented by each garden filled my being with vigour, and although I had no idea how or where, it gave me a sense of purpose, the feeling that my job on Earth was not done. I knew I had to fight to survive, that there was more for me to accomplish, that I needed to stay connected.

16

PRAYER CHESTS

After the ventilator was removed, the next few days involved practice in sitting upright for short periods and a range of other minor procedures.

I hated seeing my family suffer through this. All I wanted to tell them while I was lying there was that I was okay, just so they would not suffer, especially Louis. It was like a heavy cloud lingered over him, and I wanted to let him know that it would be okay. At one point, I touched his face and said, 'It is not your fault.' Tears welled up in his eyes, and I could see some relief in his face, but I was unsure if he believed me. There was no blame in my heart. It was an accident, and all I wanted was to see his old self again, light-hearted and naughty.

Six days after the accident, the doctors deemed it safe to move me from ICU to the trauma ward, as I was recovering much quicker than expected. The move was a milestone and brought smiles to my family's faces. I loved to see them smile, and I could see the lighter side of Louis emerge again as a cloud seemed to lift off him when he interacted with the hospital staff and visitors. I knew his old self was back when more frequently than not, I had to ask him to stop making me laugh as it hurt too much. My ribs were still mending, and while breathing was painful, laughing hurt so bad it took my breath away. The hospital staff were constant victims of his sense of humour, which brought some light-heartedness amongst the daily hospital procedures, which could otherwise be a bit gloomy. Just seeing Louis interact with those who did not always suspect that he was joking reminded me of how we first met. Many years of experience had taught me that I did not have to intervene and explain to others that he was just joking, but to simply laugh along. They eventually got it. I turned to look at him and smiled. My thoughts floated back to when I'd fallen victim to his sense of humour all those years ago at youth camp. There was no one there to intervene on my behalf back then.

I was still trying to figure out what was real in the hospital room and what was in a different dimension—or wherever this was. Dimensions blurred across one another, and the angel at the end of my hospital bed looked as real as the furniture in the room.

I could hear the hospital ward's general sounds—voices at the nurses' station as they discussed what needed to be done, a man in the next bed coughing, someone washing hands, and the food trolley moving down the hallway. All these sounds seemed to be at a base level on the ground. Some of the patients watched television and it formed a background noise to the other sounds in the general ward. The television sounds seemed to be up another level, like a different frequency. Beyond all these sounds, there was another dimension, like a third level, where I heard voices. It sounded like people praying. The speech was in Afrikaans.

I turned my head to look at my daughter and, with a slight frown, asked, 'Louise, do you hear those voices?'

She leaned in slightly, 'What voices, Moekie, the people in the hallway?'

'No, Afrikaans speaking people. Praying.' With my hand, I motioned close to my face, 'It is just here, close.'

Louise listened for a second and then shook her head. 'No, I do not hear any Afrikaans.'

I tried to focus on what I thought I heard. Yes, people were praying. The prayers were in Afrikaans, and I heard them say my name. I felt so humbled and thankful as I realised the prayers were for me! I could hear prayers for healing for my arm and my lung, prayers for my knee and back. As I focused on hearing where it came from, I closed my eyes and suddenly found myself in a busy space where many people were engaged in prayer. People were everywhere; some were standing, others were kneeling, but all of them were talking to God. The space felt free from the restrictions of gravity and specifically intended for prayer. It felt like a vast, multi-dimensional bubble where people could position themselves anywhere. Nothing was flat as we would think in terms of a room with a flat floor or flat walls.

Still following the sounds of the prayers, I noticed a small group of people positioned in a circle, praying. They were dressed in white, with cone-shaped hats, and every time they bowed down to pray, their hats would fold together, touch ends, and form a complete circle. My heart felt overwhelmed that a group of people I had never met and who did not know me would pray these prayers for me. Emotions streamed down my cheeks and my heart enlarged. I realised they were people on Earth who must have received my family's requests for prayer. As they spoke, their words took on shape and colour and, as if alive, fluttered upwards and away and danced in a wave-like pattern, up and down, up and down.

I marvelled at the glorious colours as each prayer took shape before it took off. My eyes followed the prayers, which all seemed to be heading in the same direction. Like a curious child, I felt a twinge, a curious yearning, and decided to follow a single prayer. It floated through a foyer-like prayer space into an open doorway. I followed close by as I made my way through the portal, but then lost track of the prayer I'd intended to follow. I never expected such a sight. In front of me were countless spaces with the most beautiful golden chests, like treasure chests. They were all different sizes, and each one was embossed with intricate pictures, all in pure gold. Some spaces housed several of these chests. My angels, who stood behind me all this time, moved to either side of me and watched in elation as I took it all in. One of them spoke, and he sounded thrilled. 'These are prayer chests. You have one too!'

I could not contain my enthusiasm, and I felt like a little child on an adventure, astonished at the brightness of the space and the sheer magnificence of its content. 'Oh, please, could you take me to mine?'

My angels responded with delight and pleasure and took me to a large golden chest in the middle of a space filled with similar chests. The angels stood on the sides of the chest and lifted the heavy lid. I could not wait to see inside! My anticipation and excitement were met by a chest filled to the brim with prayers in the shape of cuddly creatures, all in the most magnificent colours, alive and shining. At first sight, the prayers looked like different Hebrew letters but with cuddly bodies and tiny arms. The colours were sublime; they were the deepest, richest colours with shades that I had not seen on Earth. As I studied them, in total astonishment, I had the strongest sense that each one of these prayers was for me, and emotions overwhelmed me again.

I looked at my angels. 'What do I do?'

Still sharing my enthusiasm, one of my angels said, 'You have to pick one.'

Overwhelmed, I gasped, 'Oh, please help me to pick.' I held my hands behind my back to resist the urge to grab one.

'Each prayer is for something specific,' Pointing at a blue-coloured prayer, one angel explained, 'This one is from your grandma. It is a blessing.' He pointed at a brightly coloured purple one, 'This one is for healing.'

I knew I needed the healing prayers. I picked up a brightly coloured purple prayer and could feel the love and joy emanating from it. Little arms were extending out towards me, and all I wanted to do was hug it. I knew I could somehow cuddle the prayer into me. It was shining with life, almost glittering. I immediately pushed the prayer into my chest.

One of my angels spoke, 'You do not need the prayers here; you need to take them back with you.'

Of course! I was not broken here. My child-like enthusiasm took over sometimes, yet the angels were friendly and they beamed as they watched me experience this for the first time. I chose another purple prayer and carefully held it in my hands while the angels escorted me back through the prayer rooms to my hospital bed. With the prayer still in my hands, I admired the coloured lights that danced inside it and then carefully placed it over my left lung. It disintegrated into my body in the form of tiny, little electrical flashes. I could feel the sensation of the energy that danced through my lung, and it brought instant relief. I breathed easier. Healing.

Gratitude washed over me, and my desire to thank Jesus for this healing immediately took me back to my garden, where we usually met. All I wanted to do was express the thankfulness that was pouring from my heart towards him. As I stepped into the peaceful landscape and felt the soft grass under my feet, I closed my eyes and drew a deep breath— *How I loved being in my garden.* Simultaneously a blanket of calmness folded over me while a new burst of energy bubbled up inside me. From a distance, my eyes caught the familiar arched bridge that reached over the river, and my heart skipped a beat as I watched the space, and I knew this was where I'd met my Jesus.

And then suddenly, as if my longing beckoned him, he was there. Even from a distance, all I could see was his eyes, and it felt like there was nothing that could hold me back. I ran towards him, and as I got closer, I felt more and more overwhelmed with every step. The love pouring from him was so tangible. In a single motion, I flung my arms around his neck and nestled my face on his chest. As he wrapped his arms around me, his love, which seemed to come from every direction, consumed every fibre of my being. My emotions, unable to handle the surge of love and joy, poured out through tears. In this space, I did not need to say the words *Thank you, Jesus.* My heart's intent already reached Jesus' heart, and his presence and love already responded in waves before I even arrived in his arms. This heart-to-heart interaction replaced what I used to know as *prayer.*

As usual, Jesus took my hand and we walked across the bridge into the garden. We strolled along looking at the magnificent flowers, and all the questions I'd had were forgotten. Nothing else mattered at this moment. He was all there was.

Daily blood tests required extra patience as it became harder to locate a functioning vein in my right arm (my left arm could not be used given the extent of the injuries and the recent procedures). On this particular day, a nurse came in and explained that the hospital was trialling a new type of cannula that could remain in my arm instead of them having to fish for a vein each new day. The nurse made use of a portable sonar machine to insert the cannula, and I knew this would be unpleasant, so I decided it would be easier to simply slip away back to Jesus instead of sticking around for the event. So I did.

This was fantastic! In the space, which felt like a foyer, I recognised a few of the people. A close family member was on her knees, and I heard each word as she intently prayed for me, tears in her eyes, and I could see her heart, so beautiful. I recognised the familiar way she said Papa's name, and it made me smile. More than that, I somehow knew her intent, and it shaped the prayer before it danced up and away like before. I turned and saw my daughter's friend, Carlie. We'd only met once or twice before. Her prayer was light and simple, like a child's prayer. She talked to Jesus, but instead of a serious, solemn prayer, she thanked him for joy and healing, like it was already done. Again, her intent was so clear and pure, and the prayer shaped and danced. She looked up and recognised me and ran towards me like old friends would, arms outstretched, and we embraced. The lightness and joy she brought were so tangible and real, and I suddenly realised I knew her here. 'Love you heaps!' we greeted as she moved on.

I noticed another familiar person, their heart turned upwards, and although there were no words spoken, the prayer formed and moved with the others. I always thought there were no tears in heaven, yet the thankfulness overwhelmed me again. As I wiped the tears, I turned and asked my angels for help to get to my prayer chest.

'You know I am no good when it comes to direction.' They chuckled at my comment and cheerfully navigated the way to my prayer chest. With far less constraint than the first time, I leapt into the chest right amongst the prayers. It was as if each prayer was saying, *pick me!* I overexcitedly plunged my arms around the prayers and tried to grab as many as I could, but they slipped through.

'You can only take one at a time,' my angel explained. We laughed, and I looked closely at the prayers. I recognised each person and their intent as I looked at the prayers. *How amazing this was!* As the prayers entered through the open door, somehow, they were sanctified. At that moment, I remembered Romans 8:26: 'The Spirit also sighs within us with words too deep for articulation, assisting us in our prayers when we struggle to know how to pray properly. When we feel restricted in our flesh, he supersedes our clumsy efforts and hits bulls-eye every time' (The Mirror Bible 2012)1.

Again, thankfulness overwhelmed me, and I felt the value of each prayer, of each person who'd interceded, each one who'd had a thought of kindness, a heart turned, a good intention. Here, at my fingertips, lay materialised, all those beautiful thoughts. I picked up another brightly coloured purple prayer, and remembering the lesson from before, held the prayer carefully as my angels helped me back. Again, I applied the prayer over my lung and felt relief as my lung expanded a bit more.

I became aware of the hospital bed again, just in time to see the nurse finishing up with the needle and sticking a piece of tape on my arm. He let out a sigh and hesitantly asked, 'So, how was the pain out of five?'

I gently shrugged my shoulder and responded with a simple, 'Nothing.'

The nurse pumped his fist towards his body in a downward motion and let out a triumphant, 'Yes!'

Knowing that I had 'not been there' to feel anything, my family's eyes darted in my direction, and as our eyes met, we could not contain our laughter. It hurt to laugh, but it felt good to see my family enjoy a moment of happiness, and a warmth settled into my heart as I tried to resist the chuckles.

I closed my eyes and thought about the newly discovered prayer chests and the prayers that floated from the prayer platform. My grandma, who'd passed away years before, had prayed for each child and grandchild and great-grandchild long before they were born. Her prayers were for them to follow Jesus and for their future life partners, and it dawned on me that I'd seen such a prayer in my prayer chest. I opened my eyes. It made sense! I'd always wondered where our prayers went. If we prayed and they just remained on Earth somewhere, the evil one could get to them and destroy them. Instead, they are shaped in our hearts, and as they float into the space where the prayer chests are, they are made holy and kept safe. This is where they remain until we access them. I smiled. I had no proof, but the thought matched what I had seen.

WHAT TO EXPECT

'Yes!' A gentleman pumped both arms into the air.

'Whoohoo!' Two ladies shouted simultaneously and performed a short, hip wiggle on the spot.

It was only then I realised there were others in the other-dimensional Fibonacci gardens. I had been mesmerised by the views, the sheer size of some of the gardens—some up to 50 storeys in height—that left a never-ending supply of discovery for my curiosity. I moved from one garden to the next, through the spiral arms into the centres of the gardens and back out again to admire them from every possible angle. Some gardens coiled up with the larger spiral at the bottom, while others coiled downwards, with the larger spiral at the top. They were all different, individual, and spectacular. Gardens grew on all the curves of the spirals, and the view from the interior was like discovering a new world compared to the view from the exterior. All I wanted to do was move from one spectacular sight to the next.

Until this moment, when I heard the happy shouts.

I watched as a group of people gathered—some hugged, others jumped, and there was happy chatter and more celebratory shouts. Obviously, they'd accomplished something, and the joyous mood tingled over my skin. I smiled, then laughed with happiness as I watched them break out into dance while they clapped and sang.

Although I could not imagine anything more spectacular than the gardens I had discovered, I noticed that the garden these people were working on started to spin. Slowly at first, the spiral turned, allowing multiple views to pass by its admirers. As it spun, the garden sounded a melody that soothed and celebrated simultaneously—similar to a whale singing, but melodious and unique. Much to my surprise, the plants and flowers that formed the garden, spectacular as they were before, seemed illuminated and more alive than ever, as if the spinning and the melody energised them. It was beautiful to behold these people celebrating the successful completion of their garden. Their joy vibrated through the atmosphere, and others from different gardens joined in. I did too. We were celebrating an achievement; it was contagious and free.

I had a lot of fun. I loved the adrenaline rush of discovery and surprise, the thrill of the wonder of what Jesus was up to, and his stunning creation. I giggle now when I look at this in retrospect. At this point, I had no clue. I was too busy enjoying everything to realise that I was involved in the gardens too.

I was part of the intricate planning process, part of the creation and part of the celebration. One particular large garden involved several people I knew—my husband and kids, people in my friendship circles and connections through prayer groups on Earth—and a few others I have only seen in the gardens. We worked hard, but it was so much fun!

In particular, there was an elderly gentleman I had met on Earth years before. He wore a suit and spoke with precision, each word distinguished, his tone on the more serious side. I was surprised to see him in the garden, as I remembered him being quite stern. At first, I wondered how he would fit amongst the jubilant shouts and giggles, and then turned my focus back to the garden plans. However, I soon realised that everyone there loved him with all their hearts, myself included. We all worked with such honour and love; everyone was included and appreciated, and each person had their role to fulfil.

When the moment arrived, and the garden was completed, we celebrated without restrain. We grabbed each other and danced in a circle. Our unity and love were all-important. As we danced, we kicked our legs into the centre and moved this way and that, faster and faster. The festivity included warm bread, fruits and the most delicious red wine I have ever tasted. Although his heart was joyful, the elderly gentleman chose not to be frivolous with us crazy bunch. He loved us, nevertheless. Jesus danced in the middle of our circle, celebrating the completion of the garden with us. It was such fun!

Apart from the festivity at the successful completion of a garden, we also celebrated when sections of gardens were completed—not only our own gardens, but those of others. We celebrated a lot!

I made good use of the fact that I could venture into my garden at will. When the pain became too much, when I was exhausted, I just let go. My angels were always by my side, and after discovering the Fibonacci gardens, my garden, and the prayer chests, I was all too eager to visit again and again as I knew there was so much more.

There is one nook in a garden that I have come to visit frequently. It is not my garden, neither is it the Fibonacci gardens. I was not even sure exactly where it was, but I would ask to go there during the times I needed to strengthen because of the constant pain and exhaustion.

The first time I walked into this garden, I knew that it was different. The light in the garden did not come from the sun, but I could feel its warmth. Its white, pure and energising light flowed throughout the garden. The blades of grass did not feel like regular grass, but more like a shaggy carpet, soft and vibrant with light. I got the sense that the grass longed for me to lie on it, that it was more than alive. When I lay on the grass, it hugged me, and the light from it penetrated my body and provided instant strength. It only took a few minutes. The atmosphere in the garden was healing and soothing and in stark contrast to the hospital and my injuries.

One particularly busy day with doctors and tests, I felt exhausted. The pain was intense, and it depleted the little energy I had. I decided to escape to the garden. As I lay down on the grass, I welcomed the tranquillity and the purest white light that dissolved into me. My skin tingled, and I felt rested.

Around this time, I still scrutinised each experience and hoped to determine whether it was real or not. The discovery of the Fibonacci gardens and the prayer chests, although filled with love and light, provided no reprieve for my questioning. After lying on the grass for a few minutes, I sat up.

Jesus was sitting next to me and smiled!

'Jesus, from my list of questions, I was wondering about one thing. How come I have never read or heard anything on Earth about prayer chests or the Fibonacci gardens before?' In my mind, I wanted to know if I was going crazy.

Jesus said, 'You only see what you expect to see.'

My heart was at peace, and I smiled. I was not going crazy. I realised that I could limit what I experienced in God, which was the last thing I wanted! If I had come into the garden with limited expectations, I would get what I expected. Most of what I saw and experienced was not easy to capture in words, and there was a whole lot I did not understand. Nevertheless, I was not going to limit it or question its purpose or try to compartmentalise it. Determined to be open-minded, I decided the best way forward was to simply enjoy it!

18

NOT DOING

I had been in the trauma ward for a few days when I became aware of additional angels in the room. At the foot of my bed stood a massive angel who towered through the ceiling, and his authoritative stature made me take notice. He felt familiar, and although I did not know how, I believed he was our house angel, in charge of the family. I knew I had sensed him before. My two angels, who were always present and whom I had come to appreciate so much during this time, positioned themselves around me alongside two other angels. Although I had no idea what was happening, I could sense the atmosphere changed when the angels marched, and it felt a little bit like warfare.

The next moment, a couple of nurses wheeled a young man into the ward and placed him in the section across from me. I could feel the pain and heaviness before I knew his story. The darkness around him cowered and shivered in fear, and I suddenly understood the reason for the angel reinforcements. My heart ached for him, but I did not know why.

'He tried to commit suicide; crashed into a train,' a nurse informed me when I enquired about the young man. The compassion I felt made a bit more sense. His regular violent outbursts in the hospital ward left the staff shaken, and they called in security guards. In the past, I would have reacted to the situation with judgment, blaming him as selfish for not only trying to crash into a train but also putting others' lives in danger. I would have been concerned about my welfare and especially worried about the spiritual darkness he was bringing into the space. It was not like I could get up and go elsewhere. Yet that was so far from my mind. My heart ached for him in a way I had never known before. I yearned for him to feel the comfort and joy I could so freely experience and just wanted to point him towards Jesus. I asked my angels to take me to his prayer chest. When I looked inside, my heart sank and I felt an incredible sadness. The chest was empty.

'Nothing? No one prayed for him?'

Was there no one? No mum or gran, no family member, not even a stranger to offer a simple prayer?

I looked at my angels, and the heaviness in me must have shown on my face. All my life, I had known about God and the angels and had access to anything I ever needed. Yet here was this young man, and the emptiness of his prayer chest echoed in such contrast to what I now knew I had been privileged to have all my life.

Oh, Jesus! A chill ran across my face and gripped my heart. How on earth is this man supposed to survive? Every single moment since the accident, the only thing that has kept me alive, the one thing I could turn to, any moment I needed, was knowing that Jesus was there with me all the time. This man was in such a desperate situation, and the lack of prayers seemed to tell the story of his life. Not only did he not have any visitors, but he had no one to show him Jesus, the only answer I knew. How does anyone survive something like that without Jesus?

The heartache and heaviness of this realisation sank into my being, and I immediately actioned the yearning towards prayer for this young man. I could see the prayer form, and then, somehow, I knew that the Holy Spirit, Jesus, and the angels took care of the rest.

Tears left trails down my cheeks, and the memory of the yearning in my heart had me vow that I would never allow any of my grandchildren ever to have an empty prayer chest. It kicked me into gear, and I felt so grateful to be a grandma. One who could pray. One who had time now. The hospital bed suddenly did not matter. As I saw one little grandchild's face, then the next, I felt such peace and joy as the prayers shaped and nested inside each prayer chest.

Unlike what I was taught, what I practised and believed so many years ago, there was no warfare in the sense that I had understood before. I did not get up and rebuke the devil or the evil that had entered the room; in fact, I did not even pay any attention to it. My focus was the heart, the person. What really mattered was this young man and how Jesus saw him. I can only say that the feeling of overwhelming love and compassion that flowed from me was not my own but came straight from my Lord Jesus, and once that consumed me, there was no space for anything else. No methods or strategies or steps. Just love. And love actioned anything that followed—the prayers, and even then, the Holy Spirit and Jesus and the angels took care of it. It was not at all about me doing anything; I was just being—being available, being open, being love.

It was not unusual for a team of doctors to visit me on any given day, especially early mornings. Because of the multiple injuries (it filled a 12-page report), a range of specialists was involved in my recovery process, and constant check-ups and daily tests were part of the norm. One particular morning, my bedside was surrounded by doctors—many I knew, and the chief nursing officer (CNO) who introduced himself to me. A couple of days before, I was asked what medication I had been taking before the accident. I mentioned the meds for Hashimoto's disease and rheumatoid arthritis. Obviously, I was not taking the medication while trying to survive the first week in ICU. The CNO did not waste any words.

'We've reviewed your blood test results, and your TSH levels are within the normal range. We could not see any unusual range of antibodies either. Your blood is completely normal.'

It took me a few seconds to register what he was saying. Since the accident, I had not given much thought to the Hashimoto's or arthritis that had plagued me for so many years.

'I am not sure how to say this other than that you cannot continue any medication for Hashimoto's or rheumatoid.'

He looked a little bewildered, and I suddenly understood why. Medically there is no cure for Hashimoto's or rheumatoid arthritis, and my blood results did not match those of someone who had them, so he could not technically say that I was 'healed'. But there was no evidence that I had these diseases anymore. I cried a little while they were there and then burst into tears as soon as they left. My heart was yet again overwhelmed by the goodness of my Lord Jesus. Here I was, lying in bed, not able to do a single thing for myself, not fasting, not praying for healing. In fact, I was not even thinking of the diseases, and Jesus had healed me, without me even knowing it! Just like that! Again, he showed me that I did not need to do anything, that he had done it all. My heart melted, and although I did not think it was possible, I fell a little bit more in love with him.

The rest of the morning remained busy. Several specialists and doctors popped in and out of the trauma ward, and it felt as if there was no time to close my eyes to escape into my garden. I was regularly rolled onto my side and had to tolerate some sitting up, which was so painful it took my breath away. On top of the tubular feeding, the nurses instructed me to start eating. I did not feel hungry at all, but gave it my best. I still needed oxygen, and the nurses had to replace my IV. The culmination of all this left me exhausted, but thankful to each person involved in my recovery.

Interestingly, the common statement made by them all was that they were surprised at my recovery speed. The doctors told me about a young lady hit by a bus with less severe injuries and how her recovery time in ICU took much longer. They were all saying it was unheard of to be out of ICU so soon for someone with the injuries I'd sustained. I did not know what to say, but knew that it was not possible without Jesus. There was no way I would have been able to cope mentally, never mind physically, if he was not with me! My thoughts were interrupted by a familiar voice.

'Miemie.' I looked up into Marinda, my niece's face. Her eyes were filled with tears as she kissed me on the cheek. It was a surprise visit and I smiled.

'Marinda.'

Louis and Amarinda were there as well, and before we could strike up a conversation, the orthopaedic surgeon arrived.

'Excuse me, Maria?' he held a clipboard. 'We need to do a couple more scans on your shoulder.' My family was asked to wait in the hallway. Louis and Amarinda spoke to Marinda and relayed some of the details of what had happened to me. I later heard that Marinda had collapsed into a chair, overwhelmed with emotion as she heard about the moment I'd shared with Jesus after the accident. I understood that, as I was utterly undone each time I relived that moment too.

My hospital bed tilted upright, and the foot of the bed touched the floor. I involuntarily slid off the bed and landed upright on my feet. I immediately knew that the encounter was spiritual, as I could not turn my own body in the hospital bed. I looked down at my outfit with an incredulous stare, touched the fabric, and rubbed it between my fingers. I was fully dressed, and it was unlike anything I had seen before. It was some sort of armour, but instead of heavy and rigid, the outfit was made from flexible fabric. I looked closer and noticed the pattern of tiny hexagons made from some sort of lightweight wire. My skin tingled, and my heartbeat started to race. It was no secret that something was about to take place. I found comfort in the smiles of my angels who surrounded me, postures upright—they were ready for something. I looked around and then noticed a few tiny crawling bugs on the floor moving towards me. They were the size and shape of dung beetles. I instinctively knew that I had to squish them. I stepped forward and closed my eyes tightly as the crunching sounds made me cringe. I chuckled as I opened my eyes, and my angels nodded lightly with a satisfactory smile. I let out a deep sigh and relaxed my muscles, and at that moment, I was back in my bed.

This was not my imagination, but at the time, I did not know that for sure. My angels were real; I knew that much, but the armour and tiny bugs and the hospital bed tilting? It all sounded a bit fantastic if I had to relay it. So I did not, not just yet.

A few weeks later, when my family shared some of the emails and correspondence received while I was in the trauma ward, the bugs started to make sense. The content of one email projected my recovery process in a negative light. It was probably not intended as such and likely came from the author's own negative experience with serious illness. Still, it was utterly alien to my journey and what was happening with Jesus. My family did not relay the content, only the gist of it, but I immediately made the connection. The bugs were negative words spoken against me! Again, I was stunned at how, even when I was unaware, Jesus took care of me. My angels supported me, and I did what was needed at the time, all initiated by Jesus. My focus was on simply enjoying Jesus, and he took care of the rest. I felt so completely ashamed of all the times I'd tried to manipulate circumstances. I thought I knew what was best and tried to make sure I was doing the right thing, ticking all the boxes and ensuring I did not miss anything. All those times, I missed just enjoying being in his presence and trusting him to look after it.

This new freedom made me turn my heart towards him, and that single gesture instantly shifted me to my garden, where I walked beside him again. My heart was both a mess and delighted at the sight of Jesus as I was able to spend time with him.

For the weeks to come, this was my favourite place to go to— walking in my garden with Jesus. After the first week in the hospital, I talked to Jesus during one of our garden walks, and I said, 'I get this, Jesus. I get it now. You have done everything. There is nothing more I could do but just enjoy you.'

It was overwhelmingly evident that the one thing I had learned after I lost everything, and had nothing to offer, was that Jesus loved me and always had.

I feel both ashamed and silly now when I think that it was all so evident, and I'd completely missed it. However, there was still much to learn. After eight weeks of being bedridden, I asked Jesus about my job in Heaven during one of our garden strolls.

'Somebody once told me we are being prepared on Earth to do the job we are meant to do in Heaven. What is my job here in Heaven?'

Jesus smiled at me, took my hand and continued strolling through the garden. He did not answer my question, and I realised I did not get it at all. All Jesus wanted was to see the smile on my face. He does not need me to do *anything*; he just wants me. And I could suddenly see the chain of events from before where he so clearly showed me that it was about *being*, not about *doing*. I think it is something I will continue to learn for a long time!

After the first operation on my left arm to screw the humerus back together and get it back into position, my arm was accidentally dislocated as I was rolled over for care. The pressure on my lungs was intense while I was positioned on my side, and I could not breathe. The doctors gave me some happy gas, and it felt like forever as they tried to get the shoulder back into place. The recent surgery and other injuries rendered their attempts unsuccessful, and they moved me to the theatre under a light anaesthetic as I was too weak for another operation. Their attempts were in vain, and I was moved back to the ward.

Another specialist was called in, and the team of doctors presented us with two options for a last-attempt surgery. I understood that the pending decision on which procedure to choose was crucial, as I would lose the use of my arm completely should this attempt be unsuccessful. We immediately asked for prayer and moments later received a text from Carlie, who'd prayed for wisdom to be there with the doctors as they made the decision. Of the two options presented, we hoped that they would choose the reverse shoulder replacement. A few seconds later, the team of doctors walked back into the room and unanimously declared that they had come to a decision—the reverse shoulder replacement!

I felt overwhelmed at the instantaneous intervention of my Lord Jesus. The prayer was answered within seconds, and whether the team of doctors knew it or not, their decision was divinely facilitated.

JOY WAVES

In a blink, I slid through, and the prayer space was in front of me in all its glory. I smiled and looked at the angels by my side. With joyful anticipation, they guided me towards the area where my prayer chest was. We moved through the foyer, and I could not make sense of where anything started or ended. There was no visible roof or floor, yet doorways separated clearly-designated rooms. The place was like nothing I had seen on Earth, as there were no flat surfaces, and I could not tell if we were moving up, down, or in a straight line. As we moved forward, I watched as prayers floated by, each to a specific chest. The prayers were the most gorgeous variety of colours—some danced in, others moved a bit slower and steadier. Each one seemed precious and pure.

My angels pointed upwards, and as I tilted my head back, goosebumps covered me in what felt like a magical moment. Above our heads were millions of streaming lights, all flowing from different directions. They twirled and twisted, like dancing, and shape-shifted in wave-like patterns that went up and down, up and down. The stream of gorgeous colours saturated the space, and the way they moved completely enthralled me.

In comparison, the brightest rainbow would look like a dim reflection. These light streams were intense bursts of colour that originated from the artist's paint tubes, except they were illuminated from the inside. They were the most intense purples, soft greens, gorgeous blues, deep oranges, rose-coloured pinks, bright yellows, and so many other colours. As the balls of colour moved, their light strangely lingered and left a trail of brilliant colour shaping the sparkling streams dancing above our heads.

The light did not fade as I expected, and I could not help but think that they were happy, even joyful. They were alive! The joy was contagious, and I felt like a child in a wonderland. Never have I seen anything this spectacular. The frequency in this space was so high and intense, and I could only guess that it was a direct expression of Jesus manifesting the fullest of joy! As we moved, I stared at the movement of the waves of multi-coloured lights and how they criss-crossed and danced.

Suddenly I noticed the shape of flowers. From the angle I looked at, the waves of colour formed pictures! Could this be? To my uttermost glee, I pointed at other waves that streamed into the shape of beautiful leaves. They were not just randomly moving about! The joy was overwhelming, and my angels had beaming smiles as they watched me discover the patterns above our heads. I was sure I gawked, but the scene was all too wonderful! Not only was it captivating to watch, but just being in the atmosphere overwhelmed my whole being with joy. It felt like my body calibrated somehow to match the frequency, and every part of me seemed drenched in exhilaration and joy, shivering yet completely happy.

My mind struggled to fathom what I was seeing. The space we were in seemed so secure, as if nothing could ever penetrate it, yet as open as the sky. I realised there were no elements to contend with here, no sun or rain, and I giggled at how my mind constantly tried to find something I could compare it to on Earth. I quickly realised how futile these comparisons were, and I looked at my angels with a face that must have reflected the questions racing through my mind.

'What is this place?'

They smiled, nodded and then helped me move out of the space. We travelled fast and outwards, from what I could tell. Away, up, and out. The thrill was fantastic, and the excitement of something new was tangible. My angels beamed at me, their excitement evident. We travelled for quite some time, and then we turned to look back at the place from where we had come.

I gasped. *How do I even begin to describe this?* The *space* we had just come from, which I presumed had no roof or floor, was probably the size of a planet! There was not much in terms of *space* at all! The closest I could come to describing the shape of this mesmerising colourful, living energy is that it was similar to a spindle torus which seemed to constantly be revolving in three-dimensional space about an axis that passed through the centre of a circle. Not once, but twice! The colours moved across its surface and formed a solid, constantly flowing rainbow. It was not *space;* it was a solid world. I could only stare in wonder.

My *a-ha* moment must have been evident to the angels, as I realised the wave-like lights inside this amazing place were not even visible from where we were. The 'joy-waves' were on the inside of this magnificent world! What we looked at seemed like a protective membrane of energy, and I knew that the prayers on the inside could not be in a safer place.

Oh, how little I understood! Looking at this incredible sight was absolutely wonderful, yet the more I saw, the less I felt I knew. It did not matter if I understood or not. I mean, how do you even describe this? All I could do at this stage was enjoy the view and smile at the wonder of my Father. It reminded me of a song about his beauty beyond description and how no words could ever describe him, and I realised it was truly unlike anything I had ever seen.

My heart was overflowing, and tears streamed freely as I marvelled at the magnificence. *That is my Jesus! That is him holding it all together. That is his energy and beauty on display for all to see.* My angels slowly nodded in honourable admiration as the words from my heart took on shape.

We returned to the space where my prayer chest sat. I looked around and noticed multiple other chests, all different sizes with pictures on the golden lids—each unique and absolutely stunning.

'Are any of these my children's?' I asked my angels with a bit of hesitation, not sure if my curiosity was appropriate.

The angels smiled, almost like they expected my question. 'Whose chest would you like to see?'

I beamed and quickly responded, 'My eldest daughter.' The angels guided me through to another space with chests and pointed at one. As they lifted the lid, I felt so grateful to be able to look inside. Similar to my prayer chest, it was filled, and I recognised the people who'd prayed some of the prayers. Many of them were from my husband and me, so many blessings, and my heart felt overwhelmed as I noticed a prayer from my grandmother, who had prayed for generations to come, even before my children were born. Prayers for blessed and happy marriages, for grandchildren who would follow Jesus. Tears of gratefulness streamed down my face. I knew of her prayers, but to see them here as tangible, living prayers, just overwhelmed me again. I was a mess. I wiped the tears and asked to see my son's chest and my youngest daughter's as well. As the chest was opened, my whole body shook as I cried, so thankful to Jesus for each prayer, for each beautiful person who prayed.

'May I see my son-in-law's prayer chest, too, please?' I asked, not knowing if I was allowed. My angels, without hesitation, held my arms and comforted me as we moved along. Their support was intense, and I could feel their care and concern for me each time emotions overwhelmed me. How beautiful they were!

We arrived at my son-in-law's prayer chest, and my heart unexpectedly ached as I looked inside. Although there were prayers inside, they were not as numerous, and I realised that there were not as many grandmas or aunties or people who prayed over each person. Each prayer, each thought, mattered deeply.

I was astounded with gratefulness, and every fibre in me thanked Jesus for the privilege I had not only to see the prayers, but also to add new ones to every child's prayer chest. I would use my time in this hospital bed to keep those chests filled to the brim. I closed my eyes and started talking to Jesus about my children and grandchildren—how He loves them. Oh, how much He loves them!

Whenever I needed healing for any part of my body or relief from the pain, I went to my prayer chest to collect a prayer. I did not need the strong painkillers anymore, as my body responded miraculously each time I visited the garden or prayer chest or just had an encounter with Jesus.

Now that I was aware of the joy waves in the space, I could not help but adore the beauty of the shapes and colours, and although I visited many times, the mysteriousness and wonder of the waves never ceased to astonish me. On one occasion, my fascination got the better of me as we moved in the direction of my prayer chest. I was admiring the lights above our heads, so I stood on my tiptoe, reached up and touched one of the waves with the very tip of my middle finger. I cannot tell you why I did this except that it was stupendously beautiful to watch, and inquisitiveness has always been part of who I am.

I did not think it through, the fact that the light of the joy waves was pure energy, that the light in them was alive, and when I touched the beam, it was like touching pure lightning. Electricity shot through my being and expanded and filled every cell to the maximum with instant joy. I could barely cope. My body in the hospital bed shook and vibrated as I started to giggle and then laughed out loud. It hurt. It was wonderful. I felt light and burst with bliss as I had never felt this much joy vibrating through me, and at the same time, each broken bone and wound ached from the involuntary shaking. Note to self for next time—adore from a distance!

20

AN ETERNAL EXPERIENCE

Less than a month after the accident, I was discharged from the hospital. As Louis wheeled me out, one of the surgeons ran after us.

'Maria! Maria!' We stopped, and he caught up. He threw his arms around me and hugged me. 'I just wanted to say goodbye and let you know I've never had a patient like you.'

'It's not me,' I kept saying and thanked him for all he had done.

The nurses who looked after me continuously talked about the light and different atmosphere around us. I genuinely believe the hospital staff saw a glimpse of Heaven and felt the touch of Jesus when they were in the space around me. It really was not me. I was too busy enjoying Jesus' presence, and he enjoyed being with us. It just spilled into the hospital room. How could it not?

I felt immensely blessed to be home with my family in time for Christmas. It was more precious than any other year, and I have never enjoyed any Christmas so much—ever. We did not have the decorations and the massive feast, we barely had time to unpack, but as we spent Christmas together, we all realised that the time we had was a gift. It could have been so different if I had not found Jesus on the day of the accident. I would not have survived the first few hours, let alone make it through ICU.

My family took turns to take care of me, as I could still not move without help. Louis and my son installed an adjustable bed and some equipment to assist with showering and using the facilities. It felt amazing to be back home. The peaceful sounds of the farm replaced the hospital noises, and I adored the views of the mountain range and sunsets more than ever. Our dog even came into the room to say hello and gently put his snout on the most injured part of my arm as if to say that he knew.

Contrary to a few months before, the absence of self was an unexpected consequence of my experience with Jesus. My injuries and my road to recovery somehow never took the front stage. If I had to overcome the challenges as my old self before the accident, I would have despised every bed-ridden second, hated the circumstances, and probably wished to be dead.

I was incredibly thankful for the help I received and my family's support and time in daily things. I chuckle when I think of one specific day that was a bit more eventful.

The warm water running over me felt soothing, and I closed my eyes for just a few seconds to savour my almost independent shower time. The refreshing water ran through my hair and over my back and brought a grateful smile.

'Thank you, Jesus.' Ah, the simple joys in life! Who would have thought a few weeks ago that showering would be so enjoyable? I breathed in deeply with caution and opened my eyes. I knew the enjoyment of the shower and my body's tolerance for sitting upright had a delicate balance.

I smiled at the angels around me as we exchanged glances, and they seemed to echo the enjoyment and gratefulness in my heart. A few minutes into the shower, my breathing became heavier, and the shower chair, which provided me with some level of independence, now felt hard and uncomfortable. I needed to get back to bed, which meant I needed to get down the shower step and onto my scooter, parked away from the shower. I could not do this alone as I could not stand up. A few minutes earlier, Louis had helped me into the shower and then moved the scooter out of the way to enable the shower door to close. I could hear the clangour of tools in the shed a few metres from the house.

'Louis ....' It sounded like a puffed whimper instead of the call I'd attempted. The breath in my lungs was just enough to keep me breathing; calling out was not an option. I looked at my angels, who now stared at me with widened eyes. Interestingly, there were always two angels with me, yet when I needed to move about, there were four present. They looked at me in anticipation as if waiting for something.

'Okay.' I giggled. Despite the pain that shot through my body, I somehow found my predicament funny.

'You will just have to help me.' I shrugged a shoulder and looked at the angels. They looked at me with eyes that questioned the meaning of what I'd just said.

'Well,' I started to clarify, 'I need to get out of the shower and cannot get to the scooter. Louis can't hear me.' The angels looked at each other and then back at me.

'You will just need to bring the scooter and help me on.' The expression on their faces forced another giggle over my lips, and all I could think was how much fun this shower time was.

Widened eyes greeted my request, and one of them said, 'We are not commissioned to do that.'

I took a second for a breath and then said, 'Well, then you will have to go and get Louis.'

Two of the angels disappeared immediately, and I smiled at the other two who were by my side, keeping me upright.

I heard the front door slam a few seconds later, and Louis' brisk yet distinct footsteps sounded closer.

'I'm so sorry, I'm so sorry, I'm so sorry!' he jolted into the bathroom and helped me out of the shower.

Later, when I asked Louis how he knew to come inside, he sheepishly confessed to forgetting that I was in the shower as he had so much to do. While he worked in the shed, a clear thought suddenly came out of nowhere, *Your wife Maria is in the shower.* He then dropped everything and ran. I chuckled. Interestingly, the thought was not something one would usually internally voice to self like, 'My wife is in the shower.' Instead, it seemed to resemble something that someone else would say to him.

When the first people asked to come and visit to hear my story, I felt nervous as it meant I had to share what had happened with someone other than my family or close friends. Those close to me were comfortable with my stories, and it was not strange for them to cuddle up next to me and engage and experience Jesus' overwhelming love along with me. They also had their own experiences, as they discovered they had full access to everything I had, minus the accident. They were used to my nuances and struggles with English and forgave any grammatical errors even before they occurred. By now, they would fill in the blanks and deduce the meaning of what I relayed in broken terms, and I could speak with relative freedom. To them, the stories were not just stories; they were real, everyday events, active as much in their lives as mine. It gave me the biggest thrill!

New people, even acquaintances, meant I had to translate my thoughts from heavenly dimensions, where words were obsolete, into words that somehow resembled the experience, then from Afrikaans to English, with its multiple tenses and words I hardly seemed to remember when I needed them. It was pertinent for me to make sense, not for my sake, but for those who listened, so they would not miss out.

I was propped up in bed and could maintain the upright position for short periods before I needed to take a break. A small group of people walked into my bedroom, and instead of the stage fright and nerves I expected, I immediately felt joy and excitement that was hard to contain. My angels were excited too, and I could feel Jesus' joy. Sensing the joy and love almost made me wonder if the anticipated visit was special and if I should expect something extraordinary. I then realised they always engaged with such love and joy and every small thing—and profound thing, of course! —was met with a distinct sense of celebration. Their enthusiasm never waned as they expressed their excitement over each moment we engaged in something beautiful, experienced something new, watched us with joy on their faces. It genuinely felt as if they found joy in us discovering joy. Nothing seemed too small to celebrate and enjoy.

The urge to share with the group of people, to help them see that they were part of the story, was so strong, it dissolved my hesitation and the initial fear of blunders. A lady I have met once or twice before in our Christian circle was there too. She sat beside my bed.

I started to share about the day of the accident and the curious things that happened—the nerves that felt so foreign, my mobile phone that I'd left on the small tractor, and how I'd seen the accident before it happened. I tried to compose myself as I recalled the details of my thoughts, how I lost everything. By the time I started to utter Jesus' name, the first moment I had become aware of him, words eluded me, and I became a blubbering mess as emotions leaked out of my eyes. I could not mention Jesus' name without immediately experiencing that one moment with him in its full intensity. I tried many times and miserably failed. Still.

'I'm sorry.' I wiped my tears and tried again.

'Don't apologise. It is so beautiful.' The lady wiped tears from her cheeks and took my hand. 'What happened after you saw Jesus?'

In broken English, and with carefully chosen words, I relayed what I experienced.

'What colour are Jesus' eyes?' she asked.

The question caught me off-guard as it was not something I specifically looked for, not because I could not see his eyes, but because everything in that moment with Jesus was overwhelming.

'I don't know.' I had to catch my breath and felt frustrated both at the limited time I had to share and my body's ability to keep up with my heart that felt as if it could explode any moment from the love that I wanted to pour into the people in front of me. I listened to the Holy Spirit, carefully selecting a few highlights from the journey thus far, as I knew I could only share a fraction of what I wanted to gift them with, have them grasp, make them see that this was not just for me but for them as well. I needed to hear which parts I should share, what was vital for them to hear. I focused on Jesus and his heart for them, and as I did, my heart burst. There was no point in apologising for the tears.

I found it fascinating and thought at first that it was a coincidence that I could sense Jesus' heart in so much detail for the lady who sat beside my bed. I could feel Jesus' love for her and an intense desire for her to engage in this love. I could see how he looked at her, how beautiful and precious she was to him. I wanted to grab her hand and pull her into Heaven, have her see how much she means to Jesus, how deeply he loves her and what she has access to, but I restrained myself.

'We have no idea how much he loves us.' I repeated and hoped that the meaning would somehow become a reality inside their hearts.

'How do you go to your garden or Heaven? What is it that you do to see it?' the lady asked after I caught my breath and had a sip of water.

'It's just here.' I indicated close to my face and almost slipped away; instead, I fought to stay conscious in the room with the people.

'But do you focus on something specific or pray something? How do you do it?'

'It's just here—I just let go. I don't really do anything but just let go. It's just to become aware of it, and then you let go.'

I heard myself repeat the same thing over and over and hoped they would understand it. The lack of steps, the absence of procedures and formulas, the simplicity of simply engaging with Jesus, that was all there was to it. There truly was only one thing—his love. It was not about seeking experiences at all. Experiences did not help me discover Jesus' love; his love became everything, and the experiences resulted from that love. I did not know if they got the idea that looking for adventure was not the goal. I could not care less if I never had another experience in my entire life, as long as I had Jesus, as long as I could feel his love.

'If you want an experience, then dive the Great Barrier Reef. That is a great experience!'

When the next group came to visit, and the group after that one, I realised that Jesus' heart for each individual poured through my soul and that it was not a one-off coincidence. It is the warmest and most shattering experience all in one. The intense desire to share the love that my physical body could not possibly endure for more than a few seconds and the overwhelming beauty of the person in front of me—the way Jesus sees them, left me overwhelmed each time. Without exception, this was true for each person. I have not met a single person who he does not love in a way that astonishes me.

Moments with Jesus continued to bring healing to my body. My strength grew, and in a few weeks, I managed to go from full assistance to getting up from bed and around via a scooter to short independent walks, even if it was just from my bed to the chair. Despite the daily struggles, healing was never my sole focus. After completing routine tasks such as showering or eating, I could not wait to get back to Jesus. The times in between always seemed too long, and I would run to him each time as if we had not seen each other for days, even though it was barely an hour ago. I remained consumed by the impact the moment with Jesus after the accident had on me, and his love kept drawing me back to him. Consequently, my focus was always on Jesus, what he was doing, where he was taking me, what he was showing me. My focus was on him, and his love and the time I spent with him translated into some of the experiences that continue today.

I wanted everyone I knew to engage with what was available to them, to understand how loved they were. A few weeks into my recovery,

I called a person and asked them to sit beside me. I started to share, and the person immediately put their hand up and stopped me.

'I am dealing with a lot of emotional issues at the moment. I do not have the space to listen to your story.'

I felt gutted, not for me, but for this person. My heart wanted this person to discover what was available to them, know the love Jesus has for them, and find healing for all their hurts. Instead, this person wanted nothing to do with it. It was tough, but I realised that even Jesus does not force anyone; we all have free will to choose. He does not love anyone less because we do not choose him or engage with him. Honestly, it would be such a loss not to engage with his love as I could not imagine life without the freedom and love I now enjoy. Gone were the days when I searched for the next new thing, the correct method, for a better strategy. Back then, I worked harder and harder at being a better Christian, doing more for God, hoping that I would be loved; while all this time I could not be loved any more than I already was. I just had not discovered it or engaged in it before.

Another situation presented itself a few weeks later when other people arrived to visit, and I had the same desire to share with them as I'd had before, the same overwhelming love of Jesus for them. However, I could sense scepticism, and it felt as if they filtered the events as I talked, and it lessened the impact severely. When I shared what I perceived would be good, instead of the usual inquisitive questions about Jesus or the dimensions, they wanted to pray for me and said that sickness was not from God and that God commanded them as believers to lay hands on the sick.

At that moment, I heard my old self, and for the first time, saw the resistant religious views I once held so dear. Back then, I would have looked at the situation the same way they did—the next healing project, the next thing I had to do because I was commanded to. They prayed, and I cringed. Their prayer demanded I be healed, and I could not marry it up with anything I had experienced with Jesus over the previous few weeks.

Here I shared the gut-wrenching journey of love that forever changed me, the miraculous survival of the accident, the above-expected tempo of recovery, the inexplicable healing of my Hashimoto's and rheumatoid arthritis, and beyond that, the all-access connection available to anyone who wants it, and the response was a 'let me add to it'. That is what it felt like.

I realised how many times I must have missed the love, the open arms, the fellowship, and joy that Jesus offered and instead traded it for something I had to do. Some goals to accomplish, some tasks to complete. I exchanged it for religion—stubborn, I-know-better religion.

It took me some time to realise that it was not my job to connect everyone, change their perspective, or convince them of what was true for them. I looked at Jesus, who, despite rejection, continued to love. Although my heart would ache for each beautiful individual, all I could do was honour their free will.

A dear couple I care for deeply came to visit as well. It was the first time they'd seen me since the accident. Despite the husband's non-religious views—on several occasions, he has expressed that he does not believe in God—I felt the same desire to share Jesus' love with them. Previously, I might have hesitated as I did not wish to offend anyone, or I might have thought that I should convince him, but this was different. I just wanted them to feel loved. I shared a bit and the wife teared up as she talked about her own near-death experience and that she too experienced this incredible peace and light at the time. I cried, of course, and shared more of Jesus. The husband's tears showed that he was touched, and, once again, I was left astounded by the impact of Jesus' love, no matter the person's history or views.

When someone gave me permission to look into their eyes, I could see a garden—like the time in ICU when I accidentally found myself in Amarinda's garden but had no clue where I was until later. I would always be astonished at the garden's layout, the landscaping, the unique plants and flowers, the trees, even sometimes a swing—all were as unique as the individual in front of me. Not once have I found a garden that looked similar to another. I could not compare one to another, and it was an even more significant challenge to describe what I saw. None of the flowers or plants could be found on Earth. Sure, some slightly resembled flowers on Earth, but it would be like comparing an intrinsic three-dimensional, living creation with a colourless two-dimensional picture. What made it even harder was when I tried to explain that their garden was living and I would say, 'not like on Earth, it is really alive.' How would you describe flowers and plants that have a light of their own, that felt as if they had personalities of their own, that they were living beings specifically planted in that particular spot in the garden?

I was a teary mess each time I looked into someone's eyes and then felt taxed with trying to describe what I saw. Each time I felt so privileged and was overwhelmed by the sheer beauty and stunning arrangements. It took a lot to compose myself. At one point, I just said that it hurt too much to look into people's gardens. It was all-consuming, so I refrained from this for a while.

At first, I thought that the gardens I saw in people's eyes were their gardens, like my garden I regularly visit. But later, I started to believe this was how Jesus viewed the person and that the overwhelming beauty and preciousness he saw in that person is what he allowed me to see. It makes each person so special and unique, and it touched my heart to know how much Jesus cared about each individual. He sees beauty when he looks at each one.

Tiny, yet excruciating arm movements, formed part of the exercise regime of the weekly physio sessions. On one particular day, my regular nurse was not available to come to our home, and a substitute nurse, a young lady, introduced herself as she walked into my bedroom.

'Hi, I am …' She froze at the end of the bed and stared at me with a perplexed look.

'Hello, I'm Maria.' I motioned towards the chair next to my bed, as I hoped it would ease the obvious awkwardness.

'I know you!' The nurse walked towards the chair and put her bag down before she slowly sat down. She stared at me with a look of disbelief, which added to the uneasiness.

'Umm, I don't remember you?' I attempted a smile, but my statement sounded more like a question that needed a response.

'Yes, it was you! You were there to help us in December at Noosa. You came just at the right time—you, with your face and your accent. It was you. I am sure.'

'Umm. No… Umm, it couldn't have been me. I was in hospital in December. I had a really bad accident and can still not move.'

Her shoulders dropped slightly, and the nurse sighed, tilted her head to the side, and frowned. She leaned forward and looked me in the eyes. 'I'm sorry. You must think that I am completely crazy, but I'm certain it really was you. You came to help.' She looked down and shook her head. As if startled, she sat up straight, reached out, and gently touched my arm. 'Sorry, I am here to do the physio for you. Let's get started.'

Long after the physio session ended, my mind mulled over her assuredness that it was indeed me she remembered. It left me perplexed, and I decided just to allow it to drift along with all the other adventures I could not make sense of yet.

Months later, Louise and her husband, Henry, went to Vietnam on a short trip. There is a three-hour time difference between Australia and Vietnam, and while it was a habit for us to make contact each morning to talk about life and what was happening with Jesus, it was still early in Vietnam, so I decided to text her.

Each night I had dreams where our group of close friends and some family were involved in helping people or doing something with Jesus. It seemed very real, but I could not know if the dreams were like my other experiences with Jesus or just dreams. Not for sure.

The text message I sent to my daughter asked if she remembered anything interesting from the previous night. I watched the three dots bob up and down as she typed in Messenger, and my heart burst as the messages came through one after the other. Then I could not help but squeal! She relayed the previous night's spiritual events in detail exactly as I remembered them too! She was there, and she remembered, which meant it was not my imagination! It was real! And it was stunning to think that we were in different time zones, yet Jesus brought us together in the same place during our sleep. I was overjoyed.

I was then reminded of the physio nurse and her insistence that I had helped them in December, and I realised that we could be in any given place with Jesus no matter where we were physically on earth. It was too wonderful, and for the rest of the day, I was an emotional mess and kept thanking Jesus, even though I did not understand it fully.

Despite warnings from the team of doctors, nurses, and physios that I would have minimal movement in my left arm, severe limitations on what I would be able to resume physically, and permanent disability, I have grown stronger each day. For one thing, I was told that I would never be able to hang washing as I would not be able to lift my left arm by much and that, best-case scenario, I would be able to do a maximum of eight hours of work a week on the computer. As I write this, nearly four years since the accident, my hospital check-ups continue to surprise the staff, and I have regained movement in my left arm beyond expectation. Yes! I do hang washing and my work hours average full-time, including physical work and computer work.

Recently, I returned from town with the ute and stopped to close the farm gate behind me. Usually, I would turn the engine off and leave the ute in gear, but instead, I pulled the handbrake as far as I could manage. When I heard the crunch of gravel, I realised too late that the ute had started to roll backward. I stood and watched as it made its way past me as I held the gate open, and then discovered that I could indeed run! I made my way around the ute and jumped into the driver's seat and hit the brakes. Somehow the handbrake had not functioned properly. After the ute came to a stop and all was fine, I had a good laugh. I was puffed but thrilled that I'd managed to run and jump!

If you passed me by as I go about my usual business, you would be none the wiser. Also, despite the specialists' predictions that Hashimoto's and rheumatoid arthritis would return, my blood test results continue to come back in the normal range, and I enjoy a life free of pain.

I am just a regular person, like you. I once tried exceptionally hard to prove I was good enough, and nothing good came from that. Then I saw Jesus, not as I thought he was, but how he has always been. I experienced his love, and it reset all I had ever known. Besides the never-ending desire to continually spend time with Jesus, there is nothing I enjoy more than seeing someone else discover Jesus' love.

The Moment in Jesus's Arms

On that day in 2017, in a fleeting moment, everything was snapped away from me. The tree struck me, and I not only struggled with excruciating pain, but for the first time in my life, I was utterly powerless. No plan I could make would find a way out of this horror or change the course of events; neither was I afforded a simple adjustment in the hope that events might go my way. Admitting my helplessness paved the road towards the grievous inevitability I did not want to face—that this dreadful road I was forced to venture down would end in certain death.

Amongst the scurry of medics, the engine sounds of the ambulances, and the helicopter, I grappled with the awful sounds escaping from my chest and the reality that I desperately needed help. Perhaps death presented as such a terrifying notion because of the unknown; maybe it was because I had no control over any part of it whatsoever. Either way, the help I longed for was not from the medics, since there was not much they could do for me. Independence accentuated my life, and there were few things I would not hesitate to tackle alone but to die—*that* I could not face by myself. I needed Jesus. Desperately.

'Jesus!' I called through the gargled sounds, even if it was the last name that would ever pass over my lips. I called and waited in agony.

It would have been perfect to say that I immediately saw Jesus, that I could hear him speak my name or feel his comforting touch, but I did not. Tremendous pain engulfed me. I focused on my breathing, slowly drew air into my punctured lung, and tried to remain very still.

Out of nowhere, I was presented with the question, 'Do you choose to live or die?' It came to me three times, and three times I chose to live before I surrendered everything I knew, everything I was, everything my life amounted to, and I let go.

Then I saw Jesus.

This is the one moment I have returned to, that I have continually referred to throughout my journey. It is both the crescendo and implosion of all that existed for me, everything I knew, the instance that rebooted everything for me—my reset-button moment.

Jesus stood by my side and the world's existence no longer mattered. I anticipated my body being transformed into a glorious, perfect body and moving towards a tunnel of light, something similar to other accounts of near-death experiences, but none of that happened. I suddenly realised that I felt no pain. Although that was wonderful, I assumed what I experienced was still on Earth, that I was still me because I was covered in mud, my body bloody and broken from the injuries, and parts of me bare as the medical staff cut through my clothes to try and save me.

When I saw Jesus for the first time, I was not, as I had always imagined, dressed in a pure white dress, perfectly groomed and smiling. I was dirty and broken, and I felt ashamed and self-conscious. I was… just me. I was a mess, and the God of the universe stood by my side. This was not the way it was meant to be, or was it?

All of this happened in an instant, and if I could measure the events in time, I would not have given a split-second thought to my body or the lack of pain or where I was or what should have happened next or not. I was too overwhelmed, wholly immersed, and mesmerised at the sight of Jesus.

And then, Jesus did something that meant so much more to me than I could ever explain—he bent down, picked me up and cuddled me close. He picked up my broken, bloody, naked body, yet he showed no disgust for the wreck I was. Jesus kissed me on my shoulder and left arm, broken side and right knee—all my injured parts. When I called his name, I would have been content, thrilled even, had Jesus simply stood by my side, just present as I died, but he chose to pick me up and held me closer than I have ever been held.

I did not know what to do with my shame and self-consciousness at first, but as Jesus cuddled me, it felt as if I melted into his being. I looked up into his eyes. In an instant, his presence consumed me. He wrapped me in his love, his complete and total unconditional love and acceptance. Him—it was all that existed. There was nothing else I could see but his eyes. Jesus was so glorious, so beautiful. Immeasurable iridescent light radiated out of him, impossibly bright yet gentle as it washed over me and into me. Jesus was more brilliant than any light I have seen before, and his brightness was around me and part of me. Pure light in vivid colours came from him like a million waves, all flowing and rolling simultaneously, yet all that my eyes experienced was pure light—not one colour, no single feature that I could describe more than his love for me. He was all-consuming light and love.

As I looked into his eyes, I felt incredibly special, entirely and unconditionally loved—me, with my broken body, but also me from my broken past. For the first time, I realised he loved me for who I was. He loved my being, my spirit, my soul, my body, the 'me' he'd created. I could feel he loved all of me! It felt as if all the love in the universe was contained in this one moment, and all of it was focused entirely on me, like an ocean of love that poured into me! Although it was completely unfathomable, it was the most blissful experience I had ever had, and I realised that up to this point, I had no idea what love truly was. The indescribable love Jesus had for me exceeded far beyond my wildest dreams. If I could imagine impossible love and multiplied it by a million, it would still not come close to how much he loves me.

As if it was not already too profound to comprehend, with his next breath, his love consumed all I had ever done, my good works, my pride, my past efforts, my iniquities and limitations, all the restrictions I'd placed on myself, my worst fears, my rejection and every bit of darkness and doubt inside of me. All of this took place in the blink of an eye. Every bit of shame and self-consciousness disappeared.

My being felt unrestricted, free, and transformed by Jesus' love. My awareness shifted as Jesus reflected what he saw in me. I was filled with love and acceptance, with pure light. I was beautiful to him. He treasured me and loved me. The King of Kings, the Lord of the Universe, truly loved me! He held me close, like a treasure, as if I was the most precious thing in all of existence. I never knew that someone could love me this much, never understood who I was to him. I wept openly, completely consumed by his love; my heart overflowed with gratitude for this love and grace that came without condition, without reservation. I was entirely loved and beautifully overwhelmed, broken yet complete.

I sensed that this incomprehensible love of Jesus that was there for me, was there for each person, that the love he had for us was eternal. There truly is no measure for it. And this was the moment I attempted to capture when I said, 'We have no idea how much he loves us.' We see 'God is love' draped over church lecterns, we hear it being read and spoken, but something like this was beyond what I could ever imagine.

Up to this point, we did not communicate with words, but all of what Jesus shared was from heart to heart. What makes it hard to describe is that I have to take a moment that contains an eternity of immeasurable content, transpired in an instant in a perfect heavenly world via the heart, and then squeeze it through my mind and limit it to broken language and words.

The helicopter took off, and Jesus did not let go of me. He held me in his arms while we remained somewhere above the helicopter. I do not remember ever getting into the helicopter, as my focus was Jesus and him alone. I became aware that we were no longer on the farm, as I noticed city buildings and knew we were in Brisbane. I was not sure what to say and thought about the frankincense and oils I had been using for Hashimoto's and rheumatoid arthritis, and then said, 'I've used a lot of oils lately.'

Jesus smiled at me and simply said, 'Me too.'

At that point, I could sense that I would be back in my body soon. The helicopter was landing.

While I was in ICU and walking with Jesus in my garden, I talked to him about the accident as I could not understand why he lingered before he came to me.

'Jesus, why did you not come when I first called you?'

He said, 'I was there all the time.' There was so much love in his voice and tenderness in the way he said those words. His answer astounded me as I realised he was there before the accident. He was there when I called him after the tree hit me, and he was there the moment I became aware of him. The only variable that changed was my awareness of him. His presence remained constant.

I did not say a better prayer. I did not fast. I did not do anything to have Jesus turn up when I needed him. He was there all the time. He was just as present with me, enjoying the cup of coffee and sunrise earlier that morning as he was when I called out to him.

I often speak of my reset-button moment, the instant when everything changed for me. If I could refer to this moment in time, it would be but a second, yet it encompasses an eternity. It is the moment that became eternity. It is not merely a memory that I recall; neither is it in the past. The moment in Jesus' arms exists as a living, ecstatic infinity that is permanently available, hence me returning to it again and again and again. It is clear and vivid and remains so. It will take me forever to learn all I can from this one moment with Jesus.

One thing I am surer of than anything—more certain than the earth I walk on or anything my senses could perceive, more real than anything else—is that he loves me absolutely, completely, and unconditionally. I know there never existed a time that he did not love me in this way. He did not change his mind about me as time passed when I did not *feel* loved or did not see myself the way he saw me. He has always seen me as completely loved, and this is what he showed me; this is what I experienced. This is what I continue to experience every day. If there is one thing I will never have a smidgen of doubt about—ever—the thing that is truer to me than existence itself, it is his love. God never had any intention of condemning me; he still does not. He just wants to love me.

When I see what God sees, as inexplicable as it might seem, I look at my past, and my history seems rewritten. Instead of seeing the girl who believed she could never be loved, the one who felt rejected regardless of learning that she was never adopted, I see a girl who belongs, one who is precious. I see a daughter of the King. Instead of seeing myself as simply trying to be good enough, someone who had to earn to exist, someone who saw good works as sacrifices, trapped in religion, I see freedom and celebration of what Jesus has already accomplished. I see a heart ignited in love, a life of abundance. Suddenly my past does not define me. Jesus does.

When I had to surrender because I had no choice, I also had to give up my ways of thinking, reasoning, whatever it was I thought I could contribute to my life—all my plans, my history, the life I had built, my family. I had nothing. When I had nothing to offer, only then could I experience the truth of Jesus' full and unconditional love. The suffering of the accident and the recovery, excruciating as it was, was fleeting and insignificant compared to the exceedingly abundant life so full of love that I received through Jesus. What Jesus has done, who he is, far outweighs anything I could have ever gone through. When I experienced Jesus' love, it obliterated my old self. No longer did I see the world by looking inwards. From that point on, I could not help but notice how he loves all of us. And once I realised how much he loves us, there was no me left. There is not enough space—literally. How do you take boundless love and light and squeeze it into a limited body, into restricted thinking?

His love showed me that he had done all there was left to do. I no longer needed to do anything to be good enough or to be loved. I just needed to be. Being. Being loved. Being me. Being who he created. His work was complete, and there was nothing I could add to it, nothing I could add to his incomprehensible love to make me more loved or more accepted or better.

As I continually return to Jesus' arms and his gaze, he teaches me to see others the way he sees them. I cannot help but be utterly undone each time I see how he looks at each person. When he sees you, he brings an eternity of love into a moment. He sees you for who you are, with all of your faults and scars. Yet he loves you despite this; he loves completely and without limit, and his love overtakes you, engulfs you, and consumes who you are. There are no gaps. There is nothing left that you need to fill. Nothing you can do to make him love you more or less! On a good day, I still do not know what to do with a love like that!

I became aware of him, that was all. My consciousness shifted. There were no steps, no recipe, no strategy. I let go and accepted his love.

All he wants to see is the joy on your face. As you endeavour to find his gaze, may you discover that he has been smiling at you forever, anticipating the moment joy engulfs you and finds a permanent home in you.

Acknowledgements

From Maria:

There is no one I could love or thank more than my Lord Jesus, for this incredible life, for your unconditional, life-changing love and unlimited grace.

To Louis, my life partner, who never left my side and supported me through this incredible journey, thank you for your love and sense of humour to brighten even the darkest moment.

To Louise, my eldest daughter, there was no sacrifice too big for you, especially when I so desperately needed you. Thank you for your support, understanding and all the oil and arm massages you offered in so much love and tenderness. For all your work on this book, thank you for so intently listening to the Holy Spirit for wisdom and guidance. It is such a privilege to be your Moekie. To Hendrik, Bella, Elise and Andre, thank you for all the times you gave up your mummy so she could take care of me. I deeply appreciate each and every sacrifice.

To Christo, thank you for everything you have built and adjusted to enable me to recover at home in comfort. Thanks for popping in to check on me and for all the help and support you offered Dad.

To Mia, thank you for the care, help and support.

Amarinda, together in this journey, we've only grown closer. Thank you that nothing was too far or too hard, for being there even before I could ask, for selflessly giving with love - I appreciate you!

To the incredible team of medical staff who were involved in every step of the recovery process from the medics who picked me up in the field, to the staff who looked after me at the hospital with such wisdom and care, and to the physios and everyone involved in aftercare. From the bottom of my heart, thank you for being part of my recovery story and for the life-saving work you do every day.

To each person who prayed, whether it was a simple thought or a deep-felt prayer, I say thank you for each one. I still collect and apply the most beautiful prayers from my prayer chest. A special mention to the group of people in South Africa who prayed for a complete stranger – thank you for your beautiful hearts! For each single text message and email from family and friends, thank you! To everyone who visited and cared for me, for each phone call and email, thank you!

From Louise:

To Pappa, Jesus and Holy Spirit, there are no words to express the gratefulness in my heart, for this life, for the journey we get to experience, for your incredible unity and love that we get to enjoy every day. I love you! Thank you for the privilege of penning your story through Moekie.

Moekie, we were always close, but I could not imagine anything like this, could not dream of a better relationship with my mum, my Moekie. I love you (I suspect you might know this already!), and it is such a privilege to walk this journey with you, not only to see joy and love but to live this with you. Thank you for showing us Jesus in so many ways, for choosing to live, for sharing your story and patience with my questions and for going over and over each scene to try and capture it. Thanks for being part of our lives! I love your enthusiasm, your gusto for life and the emotions that leak from your eyes every time you talk about your Jesus.

Dad, a special thank you for all the moments of sheer embarrassment that is called your sense of humour. I might want to hide at the time, but you bring a burst of fun into an otherwise solemn situation! Thank you for all your support and love throughout this journey. I love you!

Henry, Isabel, Elise and Andre – thank you for the incredible love and support you are always. You are my world, my dreams in living form, my home. I love you to the end of the moon, universe and back!

To my family and friends – You were our lifeline in times of need! Thank you for each prayer, phone call, email, text, hug, visit and support you offered in so many ways. Carlie, Fiona, Callie, Chris, Honnie – the most joyful people I know; I feel immense gratitude to do life with you. Nita, thank you for providing a loving space for Dad and me to call home while Mum was in the hospital.

To an incredible editor, Nola Passmore, thank you for ironing out the creases and for your heart to preserve the message.

To everyone who contributed to this journey, named and unnamed, thank you!

A Note About Memoir

We are deeply grateful to the many people who have walked with us through the shared journey captured in this book. As is the nature of memoir, we have told the story from our perspective. To the best of our abilities, we have told the truth as we remember it, though we acknowledge that memory is subjective. For all but one, all names are real, as are all places and events. We have shared only parts of the story for the purpose of the specific narrative this book tells. Where the story involves spiritual dimensions or other realities, these have been relayed to the best of our ability within the limitations of words and language. Understand that these events are as real or more real to Maria than the physical world we live in, and we have shared them as such.

Authors

Louise and Maria have a close-knit mother-daughter relationship, and it was a joy for them to collaborate on this book.

Louise Coetzee

South African born Australian writer Louise Coetzee earned a Bachelor of Education from Christian Heritage College. After 18 years of teaching, she unintentionally found herself a writer while capturing the incredible story of her mum's near-death experience.

Nothing encourages her heart more than readers finding ecstatic joy and freedom through her writing despite the messiness and struggles of everyday life.

Louise makes her home with her husband and three kids on the beautiful Sunshine Coast, Queensland.

Maria Coetzee

Maria Coetzee, a retired bookkeeper, lives with her husband on their beautiful waterfront campground at Woodgate, Queensland. She enjoys morning walks on the beach and, more than anything loves to see the joy in others multiply as they discover more of Jesus.

Reviews are gold to any author. If you enjoyed reading this book, please leave a rating and review on the site from which you purchased it. Thank you!

Stay up to date!

Sign up for the newsletter at **www.louisecoetzee.com**